COLLINS GEM

FACT FILE

Elaine Henderson and
William Allan

D0767780

HarperCollins*Publishers*

HarperCollins Publishers
P.O. Box, Glasgow G4 0NB

First published 1994
Updated 1995, 1996

Reprint 10 9 8 7 6 5 4 3 2

ISBN 0 00 470519-X

Layout and design by
Chapman Bounford & Associates,
115a Cleveland Street, London W1P 5PN

Printed and bound in Great Britain by
Caledonian International Book Manufacturing Limited,
Glasgow G64 2QT

Foreword

Have you ever tried to find the answer to what you
originally thought was a relatively simple question? Have
you ever searched high and low and finally given up in
complete exasperation? The Gem *Fact File* is the book
you need, with its thousands of difficult-to-remember
and hard-to-find facts. Here you will find the answers to
such diverse enquiries as 'What are the member countries
of NATO?' and 'Who were the Seven Fathers of the
Church?' There are lists of everything from phobias,
abbreviations, winners of the Booker Prize and Olympic
Games venues, to the world's ten largest deserts, the
seven liberal arts and the winners of the championships
in all the major sports. In among the hard facts are
entries on more lighthearted matters, such as the order of
the presents in the song 'The Twelve Days of Christmas',
and Victorian 'flower language'.

This fascinating little book draws together material from
nine distinct fields: Politics, History, Geography,
Religion, Science, The Arts, Language, Sport and
General Interest.

Like its numerical companion volume, Gem *Ready
Reference*, the Gem *Fact File* provides an easy-to-use
quick reference point for a broad miscellany of information that could only be otherwise obtained after consult-
ing a wide variety of sources, and as such will appeal to
everyone from trivia buffs and quiz compilers to students
and journalists.

Contents

HISTORY

GEOGRAPHY

RELIGION

CONTENTS

Politics

COUNTRIES OF THE WORLD

Country	Area	Language
Afghanistan	Asia	Pushto
Albania	Europe	Albanian; Greek
Algeria	Africa	Arabic; Berber; French
Andorra	Europe	Catalan; French; Spanish
Angola	Africa	Portuguese; Bantu
Anguilla (US)	C America	English
Antigua & Barbuda	C America	English
Argentina	S America	Spanish; English; Italian; German; French
Armenia	Asia	Armenian; Russian; Azerbaijani
Aruba (Neth)	C America	Dutch; Papiamento; Spanish
Australia	Oceania	English; Aboriginal
Austria	Europe	German
Azerbaijan	Asia	Azerbaijani; Russian; Armenian
Bahamas	C America	English
Bahrain	Asia	Arabic; Farsi; English; Urdu
Bangladesh	Asia	Bangla (Bengali)
Barbados	C America	English
Belarus	Asia	Byelorussian; Russian; Polish; Ukrainian; Yiddish
Belgium	Europe	French; Flemish; Walloon; German
Belize	C America	English; Spanish; Creole
Benin	Africa	French; Fanagalo
Bermuda (UK)	C America	English

Currency	Civil Air Reg	International Car Reg
Afghani	YA-	AFG*
Lek	ZA-	AL
Dinar	7T-	DZ
Franc; Peseta	–	AND
Kwanza	D2-	–
E Caribbean $	–	–
E Caribbean $	VP-L	–
Argentine Peso	LQ-; LV-	RA
Rouble	CCCP-	(SU)†
Florin	–	–
Australian $	VH-	AUS
Schilling	OE-	A
Manat	CCCP-	(SU)†
Bahamian $	C6-; VP-B	BS
Dinar	A9C-	BRN
Taka	S2-	BD
Barbadian $	8P-	BDS
Rouble	CCCP-	BER*; BLS
Franc	OO-	B
Belizean $	VP-H	BH
CFA Franc	TY-	DY
Bermuda $	–	–

Country	Area	Language
Bhutan	Asia	Dzongkha; Nepali; English
Bolivia	S America	Spanish; Quechua; Aymara
Bosnia-Herzegovina	Europe	Serbo-Croatian
Botswana	Africa	English; Setswana
Brazil	S America	Portuguese; 120 Indian languages
Brunei	Asia	Malay; Chinese (Hokkien); English
Bulgaria	Europe	Bulgarian; Turkish
Burkina-Faso	Africa	French; 50 native Sudanic languages
Burundi	Africa	Kirundi; French; Kiswahili
Cambodia	Asia	Khmer; French
Cameroon	Africa	French; English; 163 indigenous languages
Canada	N America	English; French; Indian and Inuit Inuktitut
Cape Verde	Africa	Portuguese (Creole dialect)
Cayman Islands (UK)	C America	English
Central African Republic	Africa	French; Sangho
Chad	Africa	French; Arabic; 100+ African dialects
Chile	S America	Spanish
China	Asia	Chinese (Mandarin and other dialects)
Colombia	S America	Spanish
Comoros	Africa	French; Arabic; Makua; Comorian
Congo	Africa	French; many African dialects
Costa Rica	C America	Spanish
Côte d'Ivoire	Africa	French; 60+ native dialects

Currency	Civil Air Reg	International Car Reg
Ngultrum; Rupee	–	BHT*
Boliviano	CP-	BOL*
Dinar	YU-	(YU)‡
Pula	A2-	RB
Real	PP-; PT-	BR
Brunei $	V8-; VS-; VR-U	BRU
Lev	LZ-	BG
CFA Franc	–	HV*
Burundi Franc	9U-	RU*
Riel	XU-	K
CFA Franc	TJ-	TC*
Canadian $	C-	CDN
Cape Verde Escudo	–	–
Cayman Islands $	–	–
CFA Franc	TL-	RCA
CFA Franc	TT-	TCH*
Peso	CC-	RCH
Yuan	B-; HY-	–
Peso	HK-	CO*
Comoran Franc	–	–
CFA Franc	TN-	RCB
Colon	TI-	CR
CFA Franc	TU-	CI

Country	Area	Language
Croatia	Europe	Serbo-Croatian
Cuba	C America	Spanish
Cyprus	Europe	Greek; Turkish; English
Czech Republic	Europe	Czech; Slovak
Denmark	Europe	Danish
Djibouti	Africa	Arabic; Somali; Afar; French
Dominica	C America	English
Dominican Republic	C America	Spanish
Ecuador	S America	Spanish; Quechuan; Jivaroan
Egypt	Africa	Arabic; Coptic
El Salvador	C America	Spanish; Nahua
Equatorial Guinea	Africa	Spanish; English; Portuguese
Eritrea	Africa	Amharic
Estonia	Europe	Russian; Estonian; Ukrainian; Byelorussian; Finnish
Ethiopia	Africa	Amharic; Tigrinya; Orominga; Arabic
Falkland Islands (UK)	S America	English
Fiji	Oceania	English; Fijian; Hindi
Finland	Europe	Finnish; Swedish
France	Europe	French
French Guiana	S America	French
Gabon	Africa	French; Bantu
Gambia, The	Africa	English; Mandinka; Fula
Georgia	Asia	Georgian; Russian; Armenian; Azerbaijani; Ossetian; Abkhazian
Germany	Europe	German; Serbian

Currency	Civil Air Reg	International Car Reg
Kuna	YU-	CRO*
Peso	CU-	C*
Lira; Cypriot £	5B-	CY
Koruna	OK-	CS
Krone	OY-	DK
Djibouti Franc	J2	–
E Caribbean $	–	WD*
Peso	HI-	DOM
Sucre	HC-	EC
Egyptian £	SU-	ET
Colon	YS-	ES*
CFA Franc	3C-	
Ethiopian Birr	–	–
Kroon	CCCP-	EW*
Birr	ET-	ETH*
Falkland £	–	–
Fiji $	DQ-	FJI
Markka	OH-	SF
Franc	F-	F
Franc	–	(F)
CFA Franc	TR-	G*
Dalasi	VP-X	WAG
Georgian Coupon	CCCP-	GRU*
Deutschmark	D-; DM-	D-; DDR

Country	Area	Language
Ghana	Africa	English; Akan
Gibraltar (UK)	Europe	English; Spanish
Greece	Europe	Greek
Greenland	N America	Inuit Eskimo
Grenada	C America	English
Guadeloupe (Fr)	C America	French; Creole
Guam (US)	Asia	English; Chamorro; Japanese
Guatemala	C America	Spanish; Indian dialects
Guinea	Africa	French; African languages
Guinea-Bissau	Africa	Portuguese; Cape Verde Creole
Guyana	S America	English; Hindi; Amerindian
Haiti	C America	French; Creole
Honduras	C America	Spanish; Indian dialects
Hong Kong	Asia	English; Chinese (Cantonese)
Hungary	Europe	Hungarian
Iceland	Europe	Icelandic
India	Asia	Hindi; English; 14 others
Indonesia	Asia	Indonesian
Iran	Asia	Farsi; Kurdish; Turkish; Arabic; English; French
Iraq	Asia	Arabic; Kurdish; Assyrian; Armenian
Ireland	Europe	English; Irish Gaelic
Israel	Asia	Hebrew; Arabic; Yiddish; and others
Italy	Europe	Italian; German; French; Slovene minorities
Jamaica	C America	English; Creole

Currency	Civil Air Reg	International Car Reg
Cedi	9G-	GH
Gibraltar £	–	GBZ
Drachma	SX-	GR
Danish Krone	–	–
E Caribbean $	VQ-G	WG
Franc	–	(F)
US $	–	–
Quetzal	TG-	GCA
Franc; Syli	3X-	RG*
Guinean Peso	J5-	–
Guyana $	8R-	GUY
Gourde	HH-	RH
Lempira	HR-	HON
Hong Kong $	–	HK
Forint	HA-	H
Króna	TF-	IS
Rupee	VT-	IND
Rupiah	PK-	RI
Rial	EP-	IR
Dinar	YI-	IRQ*
Punt	EI-; EJ-	IRL
New Israeli Shekel	4X-	IL
Lira	I-	I
Jamaican $	6Y-	JA

Country	Area	Language
Japan	Asia	Japanese
Jordan	Asia	Arabic; English
Kazakhstan	Asia	Kazakh; Russian; Ukrainian; Tatar
Kenya	Africa	Kiswahili; English
Kiribati	Oceania	English; Gilbertese
Korea, North	Asia	Korean
Korea, South	Asia	Korean
Kuwait	Asia	Arabic; Kurdish; Farsi
Kyrgyzstan	Asia	Kirghiz; Russian; Uzbek; Ukrainian; Tatar
Laos	Asia	Lao; French
Latvia	Europe	Russian; Latvian; Byelorussian; Ukrainian; Polish
Lebanon	Asia	Arabic; French; English; Armenian
Lesotho	Africa	Sesotho; English; Zulu; Xhosa
Liberia	Africa	English; 20+ Niger-Congo languages
Libya	Africa	Arabic
Liechtenstein	Europe	German
Lithuania	Europe	Russian; Lithuanian; Polish; Byelorussian
Luxembourg	Europe	French; German; Letzeburgesch
Macao (Port)	Asia	Portuguese; Chinese (Cantonese)
Macedonia	Europe	Macedonian; Serbo-Croatian; Albanian
Madagascar	Africa	Malagasy; French; English
Malawi	Africa	English; Chichewa

Currency	Civil Air Reg	International Car Reg
Yen	JA-	J
Dinar	4YB-; JY-	HKJ
Tenge	CCCP-	(SU)†
Kenya Shilling	5Y-; VP-K	EAK
Australian $	T3-	–
Won	P-	–
Won	HL-	ROK
Dinar	9K-	KWT*
Som	CCCP-	(SU)†
New Kip	XW-; RDPL-	LAO
Lat	CCCP-	LR*
Lebanese £	OD-	RL
Loti	7P-	LS
Liberian $	EL-	LB*
Dinar	5A-	LAR*
Franc	HB-	FL*
Litai	CCCP-	LT
Franc	LX-	L
Pataca	–	–
Dinar	YU-	(YU)‡
Malagasy Franc	5R-	RM
Kwacha	7Q-; VP-Y; VP-W	MW

Country	Area	Language
Malaysia	Asia	Bahasa Malaysia; English; Chinese; Indian languages
Maldives	Asia	Divehi; English
Mali	Africa	French; Bambara
Malta	Europe	Maltese; English
Mariana Islands, Northern (US)	Oceania	English; Chamoro; Carolinian
Marshall Islands	Oceania	Marshallese; English
Martinique (Fr)	C America	French
Mauritania	Africa	Arabic; French
Mauritius	Africa	English; French; Creole
Mayotte (Fr)	Africa	Mahorian; French
Mexico	C America	Spanish; Nahuatl; Maya; Mixtec
Micronesia, Fed States of	Oceania	English; several indigenous languages
Moldova	Asia	Ukrainian; Russian; Moldavian; Gagauz; Yiddish; Bulgarian
Monaco	Europe	French
Mongolia	Asia	Khalkha; Chinese; Russian
Montenegro	Europe	Serbo-Croatian
Montserrat (UK)	C America	English
Morocco	Africa	Arabic; Berber; French; Spanish
Mozambique	Africa	Portuguese; 16 African languages
Myanmar (Burma)	Asia	Burmese
Namibia	Africa	Afrikaans; English; German
Nauru	Oceania	Nauruan; English
Nepal	Asia	Nepali
Netherlands	Europe	Dutch

Currency	Civil Air Reg	International Car Reg
Ringgit	9M-	MAL
Rufiyaa	8Q-	–
CFA Franc	TZ-	RMM
Lira	9H-	M
US $	–	–
US $	–	–
Franc	–	(F)
Ouguiya	5T-	RIM*
Rupee	3B-	MS
Franc	–	(F)
Peso	XA-; XB-; XC-	MEX
US $	–	–
Leu	CCCP-	MOL*
Franc	3A-	MC
Tugrik	–	–
Dinar	YU-	(YU)‡
E Caribbean $	–	–
Dirham	CN-	MA
Metical	C9-; CR-B	–
Kyat	XY-	BUR
Namibian $	–	SWA*
Australian $	C2-	–
Rupee	9N-	NEP*
Guilder	PH-	NL

Country	Area	Language
Netherlands Antilles (Neth)	C America	Dutch; Papiamento; English; Spanish
New Caledonia (Fr)	Oceania	French; Melanesian-Polynesian dialects
New Zealand	Oceania	English; Maori
Nicaragua	C America	Spanish; Indian; English
Niger	Africa	French; Hausa; Djerma
Nigeria	Africa	English; Hausa; Ibo; Yoruba
Norway	Europe	Norwegian; Lapp
Oman	Asia	Arabic; English; Urdu
Pakistan	Asia	Urdu; English; Punjabi; Sindhi; Pashto; Baluchi
Palau	Oceania	Belauan; English; Trukese
Panama	C America	Spanish; English
Papua New Guinea	Oceania	English; 715 local languages
Paraguay	S America	Spanish; Guarani
Peru	S America	Spanish; Quechua; Aymara
Philippines	Asia	Tagalog; English; Spanish
Pitcairn Island (UK)	Oceania	English
Poland	Europe	Polish
Polynesia, French	Oceania	French; Tahitian
Portugal	Europe	Portuguese
Puerto Rico (US)	C America	Spanish; English
Qatar	Asia	Arabic; English
Réunion (Fr)	Asia	French; Creole
Romania	Europe	Romanian; Hungarian; German
Russia	Europe	Russian; Ukrainian; Tatar; Chuvash

Currency	Civil Air Reg	International Car Reg
Guilder	–	NA
Franc CFA	–	(F)
New Zealand $	ZK-; ZL-; ZM-	NZ
Cordoba	AN-; YN-	NIC
CFA Franc	5U-	RN
Naira	5N-	WAN
Krone	LN-	N
Rial Omani	A40-	–
Rupee	AP-	PK
US $	–	–
Balboa	HP-	PA*
Kina	P2-	PNG†
Guarani	ZP-	PY
New Sol	OB-	PE
Peso	PI-; RP-	RP
Pitcairn $	–	–
Zloty	SP-	PL
CFA Franc	–	(F)
Escudo	CS-	P
US $	–	–
Riyal	A7-	Q
Franc	–	(F)
Leu	YR-	RO
Rouble	CCCP-	ROS*

Country	Area	Language
Rwanda	Africa	Kinyarwanda; French; Kiswahili
Samoa, American	Oceania	Samoan; English
San Marino	Europe	Italian
São Tomé & Principe	Africa	Portuguese
Saudi Arabia	Asia	Arabic
Senegal	Africa	French; African dialects
Serbia	Europe	Serbo-Croatian
Seychelles	Africa	English; French; Creole
Sierra Leone	Africa	English; local languages
Singapore	Asia	Malay; English; Chinese; Tamil
Slovakia	Europe	Slovak; Hungarian; Czech
Slovenia	Europe	Slovenian
Solomon Islands	Oceania	English; 120 Melanesian dialects
Somalia	Africa	Arabic; Italian; English; Somali
South Africa	Africa	Afrikaans; English; Bantu
Spain	Europe	Spanish; Basque; Catalan; Galician; Valencian; Mallorcan
Sri Lanka	Asia	Sinhalese; Tamil; English
St Christopher & Nevis	C America	English
St Helena (UK)	Africa	English
St Lucia	C America	English; French
St Pierre & Miquelon (Fr)	N America	French
St Vincent & the Grenadines	C America	English; French
Sudan	Africa	Arabic; tribal languages
Surinam	S America	Dutch; English; Sranan

Currency	Civil Air Reg	International Car Reg
Rwandan Franc	9XR-	RWA
US $	–	–
Lira	–	RSM
Dobra	–	–
Riyal	HZ-	SA*
CFA Franc	6V-; 6W	SN
Dinar	YU-	(YU)‡
Rupee	S7-; VQ-S	–
Leone	9L-	WAL
Singapore $	9V-	SGP
Koruna	–	–
Tolar	YU-	SLO*
Solomon Islands $	–	–
Somali Shilling	6O-	SP*
Rand	ZS-; ZT-; ZU-	ZA
Peseta	EC-	E
Rupee	4R-	CL
E Caribbean $	–	–
St Helena £	–	–
E Caribbean $	J6-; VQ-L	WL
Franc	–	(F)
E Caribbean $	VP-V	WV
Sudanese £	ST-	SUD*
Guilder	PZ-	SME

Country	Area	Language
Swaziland	Africa	English; Swazi
Sweden	Europe	Swedish; Finnish
Switzerland	Europe	German; French; Italian; Romansch
Syria	Asia	Arabic; Kurdish; Armenian
Taiwan	Asia	Mandarin; Taiwanese; Hakka
Tajikistan	Asia	Tajik; Russian; Uzbek; Tatar
Tanzania	Africa	English; Kiswahili
Thailand	Asia	Thai; Chinese
Togo	Africa	French; local languages
Tonga	Oceania	Tongan; English
Trinidad & Tobago	C America	English; Hindi; French; Spanish
Tunisia	Africa	Arabic; French
Turkey	Asia	Turkish; Kurdish; Arabic
Turkmenistan	Asia	Turkmen; Russian; Uzbek; Kazakh
Turks & Caicos Islands (UK)	C America	English
Tuvalu	Oceania	English; Tuvaluan
Uganda	Africa	English; Kiswahili; Luganda
Ukraine	Asia	Ukrainian; Russian; Yiddish
United Arab Emirates	Asia	Arabic; Farsi; Hindi; Urdu
United Kingdom	Europe	English; Gaelic; Welsh
United States of America	N America	English; Spanish
Uruguay	S America	Spanish
Uzbekistan	Asia	Uzbek; Russian; Tatar; Kazakh; Tajik; Kara-Kalpak

Currency	Civil Air Reg	International Car Reg
Lilangeni	3D-; VQ-Z	SD
Krona	SE-	S
Franc	HB-	CH
Syrian £	YK-	SYR
Taiwan $	–	–
Rouble	CCCP-	(SU)†
Tanzanian Shilling	5H-	EAT; EAZ
Baht	HS-	T
CFA Franc	5V-	TG
Pa'Anga	DQ-	–
Trinidad & Tobago $	9Y-	TT
Dinar	TS-	TN
Lira	TC-	TR
Rouble	CCCP-	(SU)†
US $	–	–
Australian $	–	–
New Ugandan Shilling	5X-	EAU
Karbovnets	CCCP-	UKR*
Dirham	A6-; UAE	UAE*
£ Sterling	G-	GB
US $	N-	USA
New Uruguayan Peso	CX-	U
Som	CCCP-	(SU)†

Country	Area	Language
Vanuatu	Oceania	Bislama; English; French
Vatican City	Europe	Italian; Latin
Venezuela	S America	Spanish; Indian languages
Vietnam	Asia	Vietnamese; French; English; Khmer; Chinese
Virgin Islands (UK)	C America	English; Spanish
Virgin Islands (US)	C America	English; Spanish
Wallis & Futuna Islands (Fr)	Oceania	French; Wallisian
Western Samoa	Oceania	Samoan; English
Yemen	Asia	Arabic
Zaïre	Africa	French; Swahili; Lingala
Zambia	Africa	English; Bantu
Zimbabwe	Africa	English; Shona; Sindebele

* Not included on the United Nations list of signs established according to the 1949 or the 1968 Convention on Road Traffic.
† No provisional letters allocated since split-up of Soviet Union. Vehicles will therefore probably still carry the Soviet Union letters SU.
‡ No provisional letters allocated since split-up of Yugoslavia. Vehicles will therefore probably still carry the Yugoslav letters YU.

Acknowledgment is made for assistance given by the RAC.

Currency	Civil Air Reg	International Car Reg
Vatu	–	–
Lira	–	V
Bolivar	YV-	YV
Dong	XV-; VN-	VN
US $	–	–
US $	–	–
CFA Franc	–	(F)
Western Samoa $	5W-	WS
Rial; Dinar	4W-; 7O-	ADN; YMN
New Zaïre	9Q-	ZRE
Kwacha	9J-	Z*
Zimbabwe $	VP-Y; VP-W; Z-	ZW

CAPITALS OF THE WORLD
AFRICA

ALGERIA Algiers
ANGOLA Luanda
BENIN Porto-Novo
BOTSWANA Gaborone
BURKINA-FASO Ouagadougou
BURUNDI Bujumbura
CAMEROON Yaoundé
CAPE VERDE Praia
CENTRAL AFRICAN REPUBLIC Bangui
CHAD N'Djamena
COMOROS Moroni
CONGO Brazzaville
CÔTE D'IVOIRE Yamoussoukro/Abidjan
DJIBOUTI Djibouti
EGYPT Cairo
EQUATORIAL GUINEA Malabo
ERITREA Asmara
ETHIOPIA Addis Ababa
GABON Libreville
GAMBIA, THE Banjul
GHANA Accra
GUINEA Conakry
GUINEA-BISSAU Bissau
KENYA Nairobi
LESOTHO Maseru
LIBERIA Monrovia
LIBYA Tripoli
MADAGASCAR Antananarivo

MALAWI Lilongwe
MALI Bamako
MAURITANIA Nouakchott
MAURITIUS Port Louis
MAYOTTE Dzaoudzi
MOROCCO Rabat
MOZAMBIQUE Maputo
NAMIBIA Windhoek
NIGER Niamey
NIGERIA Abuja
RWANDA Kigali
SÃO TOMÉ & PRINCÍPE São Tomé
RÉUNION St Denis
ST HELENA Jamestown
SENEGAL Dakar
SEYCHELLES Victoria
SIERRA LEONE Freetown
SOMALIA Mogadishu
SOUTH AFRICA Cape Town/ Pretoria
SUDAN Khartoum
SWAZILAND Mbabane
TANZANIA Dodoma
TOGO Lomé
TUNISIA Tunis
UGANDA Kampala
ZAÏRE Kinshasa
ZAMBIA Lusaka
ZIMBABWE Harare

ASIA AND MIDDLE EAST

AFGHANISTAN Kabul
AZERBAIJAN Baku
BAHRAIN Manama
BANGLADESH Dhaka
BHUTAN Thimphu
BRUNEI Bandar Seri Begawan
CAMBODIA Phnom Penh
CHINA Beijing (Peking)
GEORGIA Tbilisi
HONK KONG Victoria
  (Hong Kong City)
INDIA New Delhi
INDONESIA Jakarta
IRAN Tehran
IRAQ Baghdad
ISRAEL Jerusalem
JAPAN Tokyo
JORDAN Amman
KAZAKHSTAN Alma-ata
KOREA, NORTH Pyongyang
KOREA, SOUTH Seoul
KUWAIT Kuwait City
KYRGYZSTAN Frunze
LAOS Vientiane

LEBANON Beirut
MACAO Macao
MALAYSIA Kuala Lumpur
MALDIVES Malé
MONGOLIA Ulan Bator
MYANMAR (Burma) Yangon
  (Rangoon)
NEPAL Kathmandu
OMAN Muscat
PAKISTAN Islamabad
PHILIPPINES Manila
QATAR Doha
SAUDI ARABIA Riyadh
SINGAPORE Singapore
SRI LANKA Colombo
SYRIA Damascus
THAILAND Bangkok
TAIWAN Taipei
TAJIKISTAN Dushanbe
TURKMENISTAN Ashkhabad
UNITED ARAB EMIRATES
  Abu Dhabi
VIETNAM Hanoi
YEMEN Sana'a

EUROPE

ALBANIA Tirana
ANDORRA Andorra la Vella
ARMENIA Yerevan
AUSTRIA Vienna
BELARUS Minsk

BELGIUM Brussels
BOSNIA Sarajevo
BULGARIA Sofia
CROATIA Zagreb
CYPRUS Nicosia

CZECH REPUBLIC Prague
DENMARK Copenhagen
ESTONIA Tallinn
FINLAND Helsinki
FRANCE Paris
GERMANY Berlin
GREECE Athens
HUNGARY Budapest
ICELAND Reykjavík
IRELAND (Eire) Dublin
ITALY Rome
LATVIA Riga
LIECHTENSTEIN Vaduz
LITHUANIA Vilnius
LUXEMBOURG Luxembourg
MACEDONIA Skopje
MALTA Valletta
MOLOVA Kishinev
MONACO Monaco-Ville

MONTENEGRO Titograd
NETHERLANDS, THE
   The Hague/Amsterdam
NORWAY Oslo
POLAND Warsaw
PORTUGAL Lisbon
ROMANIA Bucharest
RUSSIA Moscow
SAN MARINO San Marino
SERBIA Belgrade
SLOVAKIA Bratislava
SLOVENIA Ljubljana
SPAIN Madrid
SWEDEN Stockholm
SWITZERLAND Bern
TURKEY Ankara
UKRAINE Kiev
UNITED KINGDOM London
VATICAN CITY Vatican city

OCEANIA

AMERICAN SAMOA Fagatogo
AUSTRALIA Canberra
FIJI Suva
FRENCH POLYNESIA Papeete
GUAM Agaña
KIRIBATI Tarawa
MARIANA ISLANDS Garapan
MARSHALL ISLANDS Majuro
MICRONESIA, FEDERATED
   STATES OF Kolonia
NAURU Yaren

NEW ZEALAND Wellington
PALAU Koror
PAPUA NEW GUINEA
   Port Moresby
PITCAIRN ISLAND Adamstown
SOLOMON ISLANDS Honiara
TONGA Nuku'alofa
TUVALU Funafuti
VANUATU Port-Vila
WESTERN SAMOA Apia

SOUTH AMERICA

ARGENTINA Buenos Aires
BOLIVIA La Paz/Sucre
BRAZIL Brasília
CHILE Santiago
COLOMBIA Bogotá
ECUADOR Quito
FALKLAND ISLANDS
 Port Stanley

FRENCH GUIANA Cayenne
GUYANA Georgetown
PARAGUAY Asunción
PERU Lima
SURINAM Paramaribo
URUGUAY Montevideo
VENEZUELA Caracas

NORTH AND CENTRAL AMERICA

ANGUILLA The Valley
ANTIGUA & BARBUDA St John's
BAHAMAS Nassau
BARBADOS Bridgetown
BELIZE Belmopan
BERMUDA Hamilton
CANADA Ottawa
COSTA RICA San José
CUBA Havana
DOMINICA Roseau
DOMINICAN REPUBLIC
 Santo Domingo
EL SALVADOR San Salvador
GREENLAND Nuuk
GRENADA St George's
GUATEMALA Guatemala City
HAITI Port-au-Prince
HONDURAS Tegucigalpa
JAMAICA Kingston
MARTINIQUE Fort de France
MEXICO Mexico City

NICARAGUA Managua
NETHERLANDS ANTILLES
 Willemstad
PANAMA Panama City
PUERTO RICO San Juan
ST CHRISTOPHER & NEVIS
 Basseterre
ST LUCIA Castries
ST PIERRE & MIQUELON
 St Pierre
ST VINCENT & THE RENADINES
 Kingstown
TRINADAD & TOBAGO
 Port of Spain
TURKS & CAICOS ISLANDS
 Cockburn Town
UNITED STATES OF
 AMERICA Washington DC
VIRGIN ISLANDS (UK) Road Town
VIRGIN ISLANDS (US) Charlotte
 Amalie

MAJOR POLITICAL GROUPINGS
Arab League
Founded in 1945 to promote Arab unity.
Original members

Egypt	Saudi Arabia
Iraq	Syria
Jordan	Yemen
Lebanon	

Egypt was suspended in 1979 and readmitted in 1989.

Andean Group (Grupo Andino)
South American organization founded in 1969 for economic and social cooperation between members.
Original members

Bolivia	Ecuador
Chile	Peru
Colombia	

Venezuela joined in 1973.
Chile withdrew in 1976.

ASPAC (Asian and Pacific Council)
Established in 1966 to promote economic and cultural cooperation in Oceania and Asia.
Members

Australia	Philippines, The
Japan	South Korea
Malaysia	Taiwan
New Zealand	Thailand

CARICOM (Caribbean Community and Common Market)

Established in 1973 by the Treaty of Chaguaramas for foreign policy and economic coordination in the Caribbean region.

Members

Anguilla	Guyana
Antigua and Barbuda	Jamaica
Bahamas (not for common market arrangement)	Montserrat
	St Christopher & Nevis
Barbados	St Lucia
Belize	St Vincent and the Grenadines
Dominica	Trinidad & Tobago
Grenada	

COMECON (Council for Mutual Economic Assistance)

Established in 1949.

Original members

Albania	Poland
Bulgaria	Romania
Czechoslovakia	USSR
Hungary	

East Germany joined in 1950.
Mongolia joined in 1962.
Cuba joined in 1972.
Vietnam joined in 1978.
Albania left in 1961.
Agreed to disband in 1991 and form a new organization – OIEC (Organization for International Economic Cooperation).

THE COMMONWEALTH

An informal association of sovereign states, without charter or constitution but coordinated by the Commonwealth Secretariat in London. Inaugurated in 1926 and based originally on membership of the British Empire. Now, republics and local monarchies easily outnumber the realms of the queen.

Members (and date of joining)

Antigua & Barbuda (1981)
Australia (1931)
Bahamas (1973)
Bangladesh (1972)
Barbados (1966)
Belize (1981)
Botswana (1966)
Brunei (1984)
Canada (1931)
Cyprus (1961)
Dominica (1978)
Gambia, The (1965)
Ghana (1957)
Grenada (1974)
Guyana (1966)
India (1947)
Jamaica (1962)
Kenya (1963)
Kiribati (1979)
Lesotho (1966)
Malawi (1964)
Malaysia (1957)
Maldives (1982)
Malta (1964)
Mauritius (1968)
Nauru (1968)
New Zealand (1931)
Nigeria (1960)
Pakistan (left 1972; rejoined 1989)
Papua New Guinea (1975)
St Christopher & Nevis (1983)
St Lucia (1979)
St Vincent & the Grenadines (1979)
Seychelles (1976)
Sierra Leone (1961)
Singapore (1965)
Solomon Islands (1978)
South Africa (left 1961; rejoined 1994)
Sri Lanka (1948)
Swaziland (1968)
Tanzania (1961)
Tonga (1970)
Trinidad & Tobago (1962)
Tuvalu (1978)
Uganda (1962)
United Kingdom
Vanuatu (1980)
Western Samoa (1970)
Zambia (1964)
Zimbabwe (1980)

Former members: Fiji lapsed in 1987.
Republic of Ireland left in 1949.

EEC (European Economic Community)
Founded in 1957 to establish a Common Market.
Later became the EC (European Community) and in
1993 the EU (European Union).

Original members

Belgium	Luxembourg
France	Netherlands, The
Italy	West Germany

The United Kingdom, Republic of Ireland and
Denmark joined in 1973.
Greece joined in 1981.
Spain and Portugal joined in 1986.
Austria, Finland and Sweden joined in 1995.

General Information
European Court of Justice
Decides whether decisions made by the Council of
Ministers for the Commission are legal.

CAP (Common Agricultural Policy)
Aims to ensure a reasonable standard of living for
European farmers.

EMS (European Monetary System)
Begun in 1979 to assist trading between member
countries. Currencies within the EMS have their value
limited to a fixed range, calculated in terms of the
European Currency Unit, the ECU.

EIB (European Investment Bank)
Created in 1958 to finance capital investment projects
to help the steady development of the Community.

ECSC (European Coal and Steel Community)
Has abolished customs duties and quantitative
restrictions on coal, iron ore and scrap.

EURATOM (European Atomic Energy Community)
Set up in 1957 to create the technical and industrial
conditions necessary to utilize nuclear discoveries and
produce nuclear energy on a large scale, in as short a
period as possible.

**ECOWAS (Economic Community of West
African States)**
Founded in 1975 for the promotion of economic
cooperation and development by the Treaty of Lagos.
Members

Benin	Liberia
Burkino Faso	Mali
Cape Verde	Mauritania
Côte d'Ivoire	Niger
Gambia, The	Nigeria
Ghana	Senegal
Guinea	Sierra Leone
Guinea-Bissau	Togo

EFTA (European Free Trade Association)
Established in 1960.
Original members

Austria	Norway
Denmark	Portugal

Sweden	United Kingdom
Switzerland	

Finland became an associate member in 1961.
Iceland joined later.
Denmark and the United Kingdom left in 1972.
Portugal left in 1985.
Austria, Finland and Sweden left in 1994.
Liechtenstein joined.

ESA (European Space Agency)
Founded in 1975. Engages its members in space
research and technology.
Members

Austria	Netherlands, The
Belgium	Norway
Denmark	Spain
France	Sweden
Germany	Switzerland
Ireland	United Kingdom
Italy	

Finland is an associate member.
Canada is a cooperating state.

EU: See **EEC**.

NATO (North Atlantic Treaty Organization)
Founded in 1949.
Original members

Belgium	France
Canada	Iceland
Denmark	Italy

Luxembourg	Portugal
Netherlands, The	United Kingdom
Norway	United States

Greece and Turkey were admitted in 1952, the Federal Republic of Germany in 1955, and Spain in 1982. France withdrew from military participation in 1966.

OAS (Organization of American States)

Founded in 1948 to promote peace and economic development in the western hemisphere, by a charter signed by representatives of North, Central and South American states.

Original members

Antigua & Barbuda	Haiti
Argentina	Honduras
Bahamas	Jamaica
Barbados	Mexico
Bolivia	Nicaragua
Brazil	Panama
Chile	Paraguay
Colombia	Peru
Costa Rica	St Christopher & Nevis
Cuba (suspended 1962)	St Lucia
Dominica	St Vincent & the Grenadines
Dominican Republic	Surinam
Ecuador	Trinidad & Tobago
El Salvador	United States of America
Grenada	Uruguay
Guatemala	Venezuela

Canada joined in 1990.
Belize and Guyana joined in 1991.

OAU (Organization of African Unity)

Established in 1963 to eradicate colonialism and improve economic, cultural and political cooperation in Africa.

Members

Algeria	Libya
Angola	Madagascar
Benin	Malawi
Botswana	Mali
Burkina Faso	Mauritania
Burundi	Mauritius
Cameroon	Morocco
Cape Verde	Mozambique
Central African Republic	Namibia
Chad	Niger
Comoros	Nigeria
Congo	Rwanda
Côte d'Ivoire	São Tomé & Principe
Djibouti	Senegal
Egypt	Seychelles
Equatorial Guinea	Sierra Leone
Eritrea	Somalia
Ethiopia	Sudan
Gabon	Swaziland
Gambia, The	Tanzania
Ghana	Togo
Guinea	Tunisia
Guinea-Bissau	Uganda
Kenya	Zaïre
Lesotho	Zambia
Liberia	Zimbabwe

OECD (Organization for Economic Cooperation and Development)

Founded in 1961 to promote the economic growth of the member countries, to coordinate and improve development aid and to expand world trade.

Members

Australia	Italy
Austria	Japan
Belgium	Luxembourg
Canada	New Zealand
Denmark	Norway
Finland	Portugal
France	Spain
Germany	Sweden
Greece	Switzerland
Holland	Turkey
Iceland	United Kingdom
Ireland	United States of America

OPEC (Organization of the Petroleum Exporting Countries)

Established in 1960 to coordinate price and supply policies of oil-producing states.

Members

Algeria	Libya
Gabon	Nigeria
Indonesia	Qatar
Iran	Saudi Arabia
Iraq	United Arab Emirates
Kuwait	Venezuela

Ecuador withdrew in 1993.

SEATO (Southeast Asia Treaty Organization)
Established in 1954 as a defence alliance by Australia,
France, New Zealand, Pakistan, The Philippines,
Thailand, UK and USA, with Vietnam, Cambodia and
Laos as protocol members.
After the Vietnam War the organization ended (1977).

UNITED NATIONS
Founded in 1945.
The six main organs are:

General Assembly	Assembly of all members.
Security Council	15 members – 5 permanent (China, France, Russia, UK, US), 10 non-permanent members elected for a 2-year period.
Economic and Social Council	54 non-permanent members elected for a 3-year period.
Trusteeship Council	China, France, Russia, UK, US.
International Court of Justice	Main judicial organ of the UN. Consists of 15 judges, each from a different member state chosen by the General Assembly and the Security Council for a 9-year term. Sits at The Hague.
Secretariat	Secretary-General and a large international staff. Secretary-General is the chief administration officer and serves a 5-year term.

Specialized agencies of the UN and their affiliation dates:

FAO	Food and Agriculture Organization (1945)	
GATT	General Agreement on Tariffs and Trade (1958)	
IAEA	International Atomic Energy Agency (1957)	
IBRD	International Bank for Reconstruction and Development (1945)	
ICAO	International Civil Aviation Organization (1947)	
IDA	International Development Association (1960)	
IFC	International Finance Corporation (1957)	
IFAD	International Fund for Agricultural Development (1977)	
ILO	International Labour Organization (1946)	
IMO	International Maritime Organization (1948)	
IMF	International Monetary Fund (1945)	
ITU	International Telecommunications Union (1947)	
UNESCO	United Nations Education Scientific and Cultural Organization (1946)	
UPU	Universal Postal Union (1947)	
WHO	World Health Organization (1948)	
WIPO	World Intellectual Property Organization (1974)	
WMO	World Meteorological Organization (1950)	

Other agencies

UNCTAD	UN Conference on Trade and Development
UNHCR	UN High Commissioner for Refugees
UNICEF	UN International Children's Emergency Fund
UNIDO	UN Industrial Development Organization
UNRWA	UN Relief and Works Agency for Palestinian Refugees in the Near East

Members (and date of joining)
Note: Founder members are in italic type.

Afghanistan	1946	Central African Republic	1960
Albania	1955	Chad	1960
Algeria	1962	*Chile*	1945
Angola	1976	*China*	1945
Antigua & Barbuda	1981	*Colombia*	1945
Argentina	1945	Comoros	1975
Australia	1945	Congo	1960
Austria	1955	*Costa Rica*	1945
Bahamas	1973	Côte d'Ivoire	1960
Bahrain	1971	*Cuba*	1945
Bangladesh	1974	Cyprus	1960
Barbados	1966	*Czechoslovakia*	1945
Belgium	1945	*Denmark*	1945
Belize	1981	Djibouti	1977
Benin	1960	Dominica	1978
Bhutan	1971	*Dominican Republic*	1945
Bolivia	1945	*Ecuador*	1945
Botswana	1966	*Egypt*	1945
Brazil	1945	*El Salvador*	1945
Brunei	1984	Equatorial Guinea	1968
Bulgaria	1955	*Ethiopia*	1945
Burkina Faso	1960	Fiji	1970
Burma	1948	Finland	1955
Burundi	1962	*France*	1945
Byelorussian SSR	1945	Gabon	1960
Cambodia	1955	Gambia, The	1965
Cameroon	1960	German Democratic Rep.	1973
Canada	1945	Germany, Federal Rep. of	1973
Cape Verde	1975	Ghana	1957

Greece	1945	Mali	1960
Grenada	1974	Malta	1964
Guatemala	1945	Mauritania	1961
Guinea	1958	Mauritius	1968
Guinea-Bissau	1974	*Mexico*	1945
Guyana	1966	Mongolia	1961
Haiti	1945	Morocco	1956
Honduras	1945	Mozambique	1975
Hungary	1955	Nepal	1955
Iceland	1946	*Netherlands, The*	1945
India	1945	*New Zealand*	1945
Indonesia	1950	*Nicaragua*	1945
Iran	1945	Niger	1960
Iraq	1945	Nigeria	1960
Ireland	1955	*Norway*	1945
Israel	1949	Oman	1971
Italy	1955	Pakistan	1947
Jamaica	1962	*Panama*	1945
Japan	1956	Papua New Guinea	1975
Jordan	1955	*Paraguay*	1945
Kenya	1963	*Peru*	1945
Kuwait	1963	*Philippines, The*	1945
Laos	1955	*Poland*	1945
Lebanon	1945	Portugal	1955
Lesotho	1966	Qatar	1971
Liberia	1945	Romania	1955
Libya	1955	Rwanda	1962
Luxembourg	1945	St Christopher & Nevis	1983
Madagascar	1960	St Lucia	1979
Malawi	1964	St Vincent & the	
Malaysia	1957	Grenadines	1980
Maldives	1965	São Tomé & Principe	1975

Saudi Arabia	1945	Tunisia	1956
Senegal	1960	*Turkey*	1945
Seychelles	1976	Uganda	1962
Sierra Leone	1961	*Ukrainian SSR*	1945
Singapore	1965	*USSR*	1945
Solomon Islands	1978	United Arab Emirates	1971
Somalia	1960	*United Kingdom*	1945
South Africa	1945	*United States of America*	1945
Spain	1955	*Uruguay*	1945
Sri Lanka	1955	Vanuatu	1981
Sudan	1956	*Venezuela*	1945
Surinam	1975	Vietnam	1977
Swaziland	1968	Western Samoa	1976
Sweden	1946	Yemen Arab Republic	1947
Syria	1945	Yemen PDR	1967
Tanzania	1961	*Yugoslavia*	1945
Thailand	1946	Zaïre	1960
Togo	1960	Zambia	1964
Trinidad & Tobago	1962	Zimbabwe	1980

WARSAW TREATY ORGANIZATION (Warsaw Pact)

Founded in 1955.

Original members

Albania	German Democratic Republic
Bulgaria	Poland
Czechoslovakia	Romania
Hungary	USSR

Albania formally withdrew in 1968.
The military structure was dismantled in 1991 but a political structure remained.

ADMINISTRATION AREAS
Pre-1974 Counties of the United Kingdom
ENGLAND

County	Abbreviation	County Town
Bedfordshire	Beds	Bedford
Berkshire	Berks	Reading
Buckinghamshire	Bucks	Aylesbury
Cambridgeshire	Cambs	Cambridge
Cheshire	Ches	Chester
Cornwall	Corn	Bodmin
Cumberland	Cumb	Carlisle
Derbyshire	Derby	Derby
Devon		Exeter
Dorset		Dorchester
Durham	Dur	Durham
Essex		Chelmsford
Gloucestershire	Glos	Gloucester
Hampshire	Hants	Winchester
Herefordshire		Hereford
Hertfordshire	Herts	Hertford
Huntingdonshire	Hunts	Huntingdon
Kent		Maidstone
Lancashire	Lancs	Lancaster
Leicestershire	Leics	Leicester
Lincolnshire	Lincs	Lincoln
Middlesex	Middx	Brentford
Norfolk		Norwich
Northamptonshire	Northants	Northampton
Northumberland	Northumb	Newcastle upon Tyne
Nottinghamshire	Notts	Nottingham
Oxfordshire	Oxon	Oxford
Rutland		Oakham
Shropshire	Salop	Shrewsbury
Somerset	Som	Taunton

Staffordshire	Staffs	Stafford
Suffolk		Ipswich
Surrey		Kingston upon Thames
Sussex		Lewes
Warwickshire	War	Warwick
Westmorland		Appleby
Wiltshire	Wilts	Salisbury
Worcestershire	Worcs	Worcester
Yorkshire	Yorks	York

SCOTLAND

County	County Town
Aberdeenshire	Aberdeen
Angus	Forfar
Argyllshire & Islands	Inveraray
Ayrshire	Ayr
Banffshire	Banff
Berwickshire	Duns
Buteshire & Isle of Arran	Rothesay
Caithness	Wick
Clackmannanshire	Alloa
Dunbartonshire	Dumbarton
Dumfriesshire	Dumfries
East Lothian	Haddington
Fife	Cupar
Inverness-shire	Kinross
Kirkcudbrightshire	Kirkcudbright
Lanarkshire	Lanark
Midlothian	Edinburgh
Morayshire	Elgin
Nairnshire	Nairn
Orkney Islands	Kirkwall
Peeblesshire	Peebles
Perthshire	Perth

Renfrewshire	Renfrew
Ross & Cromarty and	
Isle of Lewis	Dingwall
Roxburghshire	Jedburgh
Selkirkshire	Selkirk
Shetland Islands	Lerwick
Stirlingshire	Stirling
Sutherland	Dornoch
West Lothian	Linlithgow
Wigtownshire	Wigtown

WALES

County	County Town
Anglesey	Beaumaris
Brecknockshire	Brecon
Caernarvonshire	Caernarvon
Cardiganshire	Cardigan
Carmarthenshire	Carmarthen
Denbighshire	Ruthin
Flintshire	Mold
Glamorgan	Cardiff
Merionethshire	Dolgelley
Monmouthshire	Monmouth
Montgomeryshire	Welshpool
Pembrokeshire	Haverfordwest
Radnorshire	Presteigne

NORTHERN IRELAND

County	County Town
Antrim	Belfast
Armagh	Armagh
Down	Downpatrick
Fermanagh	Enniskillen
Londonderry	Londonderry
Tyrone	Omagh

Post-1974 and post-1996 Counties/Councils/Regions of the United Kingdom

ENGLAND (1974-96)

County

Avon
Bedfordshire
Berkshire
Buckinghamshire
Cambridgeshire
Cheshire
Cleveland
Cornwall/Isles of Scilly
Cumbria
Derbyshire
Devon
Dorset
Durham
East Sussex
Essex
Gloucestershire
Greater London
Greater Manchester
Hampshire
Hereford & Worcester
Hertfordshire
Humberside
Isle of Wight
Kent
Lancashire
Leicestershire
Lincolnshire
Merseyside
Norfolk
Northamptonshire
Northumberland
North Yorkshire
Nottinghamshire
Oxfordshire
Shropshire
Somerset
South Yorkshire
Staffordshire
Suffolk
Surrey
Tyne & Wear
Warwickshire
West Midlands
West Sussex
West Yorkshire
Wiltshire

ENGLAND (post-1996)

Councils

Bath & NW Somerset	Buckinghamshire	Cornwall/Isles of Scilly
Bedfordshire	Cambridgeshire	Cumbria
Berkshire	Cheshire	Derbyshire
Bristol	City of Kingston-upon-Hull	

Devon	Lancashire	Shropshire
Dorset	Leicestershire	Somerset
Durham	Lincolnshire	S Gloucestershire
E Riding of Yorkshire	Merseyside	South Yorkshire
East Sussex	Middlesbrough	Staffordshire
Essex	Norfolk	Stockton-on-Tees
Gloucestershire	Northamptonshire	Suffolk
Greater London	NE Lincolnshire	Surrey
Greater Manchester	NE Somerset	Tyne & Wear
Hampshire	N Lincolnshire	Warwickshire
Hartlepool	Northumberland	West Midlands
Hereford & Worcester	North Yorkshire	West Sussex
Hertfordshire	Nottinghamshire	West Yorkshire
Isle of Wight	Oxfordshire	Wiltshire
Kent	Redcar & Cleveland	York

SCOTLAND

Region (1975–96)	New Council(s) (post-1996)
Borders	Borders
Central	Clackmannan, Falkirk, Stirling
Dumfries & Galloway	Dumfries & Galloway
Fife	Fife
Grampian	City of Aberdeen, Aberdeenshire, Moray
Highland	Highland
Lothian	East Lothian, City of Edinburgh, Midlothian, West Lothian
Tayside	Angus, City of Dundee, Perthshire & Kinross
Strathclyde	Argyll & Bute, East Ayrshire, North Ayrshire, South Ayrshire, West Dunbartonshire, East Dunbartonshire, City of Glasgow, Inverclyde, North Lanarkshire, South Lanarkshire, East Renfrewshire, Renfrewshire
Orkney Islands	Orkney Islands

Shetland Islands   Shetland Islands
Western Isles   Western Isles

WALES Counties (1974-96)

| Clwyd | Gwent | Mid Glamorgan | South Glamorgan |
| Dyfed | Gwynedd | Powys | West Glamorgan |

Unitary Authorities (post-1996)

Anglesey	Cardiganshire	Monmouthshire
Caernarfonshire &	Carmarthenshire	Pembrokeshire
Merionethshire	Denbighshire	Powys
Cardiff	Flintshire	Swansea

County Boroughs (post-1996)

Aberconwy & Colwyn	Merthyr Tydfil	Torfaen
Blaenau Gwent	Neath & Port Talbot	The Vale of
Bridgend	Newport	Glamorgan
Caerphilly	Rhondda, Cynon, Taff	Wrexham

NORTHERN IRELAND Districts & Borough Councils* (post-1996)

Antrim*	Coleraine*	Lisburn*
Ards*	Cookstown	Magherafelt
Armagh	Craigavon*	Moyle
Ballymena*	Derry	Newry & Mourne
Ballymoney*	Down	Newtownabbey*
Banbridge	Dungannon	North Down*
Belfast	Fermanagh	Omagh
Carrickfergus	Larne*	Strabane
Castlereagh	Limavady*	

Irish Provinces/Counties

Province	County	County Town
Connacht	Galway	Galway
	Leitrim	Carrick-on-Shannon
	Mayo	Castlebar
	Roscommon	Roscommon
	Sligo	Sligo

Leinster	Carlow	Carlow
	Dublin	Dublin
	Kildare	Naas
	Kilkenny	Kilkenny
	Laoighis	Portlaoise
	Longford	Longford
	Louth	Dundalk
	Meath	Trim
	Offaly	Tullamore
	Westmeath	Mullingar
	Wexford	Wexford
	Wicklow	Wicklow
Munster	Clare	Ennis
	Cork	Cork
	Kerry	Tralee
	Limerick	Limerick
	Tipperary	Clonmel
	Waterford	Waterford
Ulster	Cavan	Cavan
	Donegal	Lifford
	Monaghan	Monaghan

Australian States/Territories and their Capitals

Australian Capital Territory	Canberra
New South Wales	Sydney
Northern Territory	Darwin
Queensland	Brisbane
South Australia	Adelaide
Tasmania	Hobart
Victoria	Melbourne
Western Australia	Perth

Belgian Provinces and their Capitals

| Antwerp | Antwerp |
| Brabant | Brussels |

East Flanders	Ghent
Hainaut	Mons
Liège	Liège
Limbourg	Hasselt
Luxembourg	Arlon
Namur	Namur
West Flanders	Bruges

Canadian Provinces/Territories and their Capitals

Alberta	Edmonton
British Columbia	Victoria
Manitoba	Winnipeg
New Brunswick	Fredericton
Newfoundland	St John's
Northwest Territories	Yellowknife
Nova Scotia	Halifax
Ontario	Toronto
Prince Edward Island	Charlottetown
Quebec	Quebec
Saskatchewan	Regina
Yukon Territory	Whitehorse

Dutch Provinces and their Capitals

Drenthe	Assen
Flevoland	Lelystad
Friesland	Leeuwarden
Gelderland	Arnhem
Groningen	Groningen
Limburg	Maastricht
Noord-Brabant	's Hertogenbosch
Noord-Holland	Haarlem
Overijssel	Zwolle
Utrecht	Utrecht
Zeeland	Middelburg
Zuid-Holland	The Hague

French Regions and their Capitals

Alsace	Strasbourg
Aquitaine	Bordeaux
Auvergne	Clermont-Ferrand
Basse-Normandie	Caen
Brittany	Rennes
Burgundy	Dijon
Centre	Orléans
Champagne-Ardenne	Châlons-sur-Marne
Corsica	Ajaccio
Franche-Comté	Besançon
Haute-Normandie	Rouen
Île-de-France	Paris
Languedoc-Roussillon	Montpellier
Limousin	Limoges
Lorraine	Metz
Midi-Pyrénées	Toulouse
Le Nord	Lille
Pays de la Loire	Nantes
Picardy	Amiens
Poitou-Charentes	Poitiers
Provence-Alpes-Côte d'Azur	Marseille
Rhône-Alpes	Lyon

German Länder and their Capitals

Baden-Württemberg	Stuttgart
Bavaria	Munich
Berlin	Berlin
Brandenburg	Potsdam
Bremen	Bremen
Hamburg	Hamburg
Hessen	Wiesbaden
Lower Saxony	Hanover
Mecklenburg-West Pomerania	Schwerin
North Rhine-Westphalia	Düsseldorf

Rhineland-Palatinate	Mainz
Saarland	Saarbrücken
Saxony	Dresden
Saxony-Anhalt	Magdeburg
Schleswig-Holstein	Kiel
Thuringia	Erfurt

Italian Regions and their Capitals

Abruzzi	Aquila
Basilicata	Potenza
Calabria	Catanzaro
Campania	Naples
Emilia-Romagna	Bologna
Friuli-Venezia Giulia	Trieste
Lazio	Rome
Liguria	Genoa
Lombardy	Milan
Marche	Ancona
Molise	Campobasso
Piedmont	Turin
Puglia	Bari
Sardinia	Cagliari
Sicily	Palermo
Trentino-Alto Adige	Trento/Bolzano
Tuscany	Florence
Umbria	Perugia
Valle d'Aosta	Aosta
Veneto	Venice

Japanese Regions/Prefectures and their Capitals

Region	Prefecture	Capital
Chubu	Aichi	Nagoya
	Fukui	Fukui
	Gifu	Gifu
	Ishikawa	Kanazawa

Region	Prefecture	Capital
	Nagano	Nagano
	Niigata	Niigata
	Shizuoka	Shizuoka
	Toyama	Toyama
	Yamanashi	Kofu
Chugoku	Hiroshima	Hiroshima
	Okayama	Okayama
	Shimane	Matsue
	Tottori	Tottori
	Yamaguchi	Yamaguchi
Hokkaido	Hokkaido Territory	Sapporo
Kanto	Chiba	Chiba
	Gumma	Maebashi
	Ibaraki	Mito
	Kanagawa	Yokohama
	Saitama	Urawa
	Tochigi	UtsonomiyaKinki
Hyogo	Kobe	
	Mie	Tsu
	Nara	Nara
	Shiga	Otsu
	Wakayama	Wakayama
Kyushu	Fukuoka	Fukuoka
	Kagoshima	Kagoshima
	Kumamoto	Kumamoto
	Miyazaki	Miyazaki
	Nagasaki	Nagasaki
	Oita	Oita
	Saga	Saga
Ryukyu	Okinawa	Naha
Shikoku	Ehime	Matsuyama
	Kagawa	Takamatsu
	Kochi	Kochi
	Tokushima	Tokushima

Region	Prefecture	Capital
Tohoku	Akita	Akita
	Aomori	Aomori
	Fukushima	Fukushima
	Iwate	Morioka
	Miyagi	Sendai
	Yamagata	Yamagata
Metropolis		
Tokyo		Tokyo
Urban Prefectures		
	Kyoto	Kyoto
	Osaka	Osaka

New Zealand Islands Regional Councils

Auckland (NI)
Bay of Plenty (NI)
Canterbury (SI)
Gisborne (NI)
Hawkes Bay (NI)
Manawatu-Wanganui (NI)
Nelson-Marlborough (SI)
Northland (NI)
Otago (SI)
Southland (SI)
Taranaki (NI)
Waikato (NI)
Wellington (NI)
West Coast (SI)
Chatham Islands
Offshore Islands
Stewart Islands

NI = North Island; SI = South Island

Portuguese Districts

District capitals have the same name as their district.

Aveiro
Beja
Braga
Braganca
Castelo Branco
Coimbra
Evora
Faro
Guarda
Leiria
Lisboa (Lisbon)
Portalegre
Porto
Santarem
Setubal
Viana do Castelo
Vila Real
Viseu

Spanish Autonomous Communities

	Capital
Andalucia	Seville
Aragon	Zaragoza
Asturias	Oviedo
Baleares	Palma de Mallorca
Canarias	Santa Cruz de Tenerife
Cantabria	Santander
Castilla la Mancha	Toledo
Castilla y Leon	Valladolid
Cataluna	Barcelona
Extremadura	Merida
Galicia	Santiago de Compostela
La Rioja	Logrono
Madrid	Madrid
Murcia	Murcia
Navarra	Pamplona
Pais Vasco	Vitoria
Valencia	Valencia

States of the United States of America

State	Capital	Abbrev	Postal Abbrev	Nickname
Alabama	Montgomery	Ala	AL	Yellowhammer State
Alaska	Juneau	Alas	AK	Last Frontier
Arizona	Phoenix	Ariz	AZ	Grand Canyon State
Arkansas	Little Rock	Ark	AR	The Natural State
California	Sacramento	Calif	CA	Golden State
Colorado	Denver	Colo	CO	Centennial State

State	Capital	Abbrev.	Postal Abbrev.	Nickname
Connecticut	Hartford	Conn	CT	Constitution State
Delaware	Dover	Del	DE	Diamond State
Florida	Tallahassee	Fla	FL	Sunshine State
Georgia	Atlanta	Ga	GA	Peach State
Hawaii	Honolulu		HI	Aloha State
Idaho	Boise		ID	Gem State
Illinois	Springfield	Ill	IL	Land of Lincoln
Indiana	Indianapolis	Ind	IN	Hoosier State
Iowa	Des Moines	Ia	IA	Hawkeye State
Kansas	Topeka	Kan	KS	Sunflower State
Kentucky	Frankfort	Ky	KY	Bluegrass State
Louisiana	Baton Rouge	La	LA	Pelican State
Maine	Augusta	Me	ME	Pine Tree State
Maryland	Annapolis	Md	MD	Old Line State
Massachusetts	Boston	Mass	MA	Bay State
Michigan	Lansing	Mich	MI	Great Lakes State
Minnesota	St Paul	Minn	MN	North Star State
Mississippi	Jackson	Miss	MS	Magnolia State
Missouri	Jefferson City	Mo	MO	Show Me State
Montana	Helena	Mont	MT	Treasure State
Nebraska	Lincoln	Nebr	NB	Cornhusker State
Nevada	Carson City	Nev	NV	The Silver State
New Hampshire	Concord		NH	Granite State
New Jersey	Trenton		NJ	Garden State
New Mexico	Santa Fe	NMex	NM	Land of Enchantment

State	Capital	Abbrev.	Postal Abbrev.	Nickname
New York	Albany		NY	Empire State
North Carolina	Raleigh		NC	Tar Heel State
North Dakota	Bismarck	NDak	ND	Peace Garden State
Ohio	Columbus		OH	Buckeye State
Oklahoma	Oklahoma City	Okla	OK	Sooner State
Oregon	Salem	Oreg	OR	Beaver State
Pennsylvania	Harrisburg	Pa	PA	Keystone State
Rhode Island	Providence		RI	The Ocean State
South Carolina	Columbia		SC	Palmetto State
South Dakota	Pierre	SDak	SD	Mount Rushmore State
Tennessee	Nashville	Tenn	TN	Volunteer State
Texas	Austin	Tex	TX	Lone Star State
Utah	Salt Lake City		UT	Beehive State
Vermont	Montpelier	Vt	VT	Green Mountain State
Virginia	Richmond	Va	VA	The Old Dominion State
Washington	Olympia	Wash	WA	Evergreen State
West Virginia	Charleston	WVa	WV	Mountain State
Wisconsin	Madison	Wis	WI	Badger State
Wyoming	Cheyenne	Wyo	WY	Equality State/ Cowboy State

History

CHINESE DYNASTIES

Name of Dynasty	Date	Capital City
Shang	c. 16th–11thC BC	Yanshi
		Zhengzhou
		(Chengchow)
		Anyang
Zhou (Chou)	11thC BC–256 BC	Xi'an (Sian) to 771 BC
Western Zhou	11thC BC–771 BC	
Spring and Autumn Period	722–481 BC	Luoyang (Loyang) 770–256 BC
Warring States	480–221 BC	
Qin (Ch'in)	221–206 BC	Xi'an (Sian)
Han	206 BC–AD 220	
Western Han	206 BC–AD 9	Xi'an (Sian)
Eastern Han	AD 25–220	Luoyang (Loyang)
Three Kingdoms	220–65	Luoyang (Loyang) Chengdu (Chengtu) Nanjing (Nanking)
Six Dynasties	265–589	
Sui	589–618	Xi'an (Sian)
Tang (T'ang)	618–906	Xi'an (Sian)
Five Dynasties	907–60	

Name of Dynasty	Date	Capital City
Song (Sung)	960–1279	
Northern Song	960–1126	Kaifeng
Southern Song	1127–1279	Hangzhou (Hangchow)
Yuan (Yüan) – Mongols	1279–1368	Beijing (Peking)
Ming	1368–1644	Nanjing (Nanking) 1368–1402 Beijing (Peking) 1402–1644
Qing (Ch'ing) – Manchus	1644–1911	Beijing (Peking)
Republic	1911–49	Beijing (Peking) to 1927 Nanjing (Nanking) 1927–49
People's Republic	1949–	Beijing (Peking)
First Five-year Plan	1952–7	
Great Leap Forward	1955–9	
Cultural Revolution	1966–9	

ROMAN EMPERORS

Augustus	27 BC–AD 14
Tiberius	14–37
Gaius (Caligula)	37–41
Claudius	41–54
Nero	54–68
Galba	68–9
Otho	69
Vitellius	69

Vespasian	69–79
Titus	79–81
Domitian	81–96
Nerva	96–8
Trajan	98–117
Hadrian	117–38
Antoninus Pius	138–61
Marcus Aurelius and Lucius Verus	161–9
Marcua Aurelius alone	169–77
Marcus Aurelius and Commodus	177–80
Commodus alone	180–92
Pertinax	193
Didius Julianus	193
Septimius Severus alone	193–8
Septimius Severus and Antoninus (Caracalla)	198–209
Septimius Severus, Antoninus (Caracalla) and Geta	209–11
Antoninus (Caracalla) and Geta	211–12
Antoninus (Caracalla) alone	212–17
Macrinus alone	217–18
Macrinus and Diadumenianus	218
Antoninus (Elagabalus)	218–22
Alexander Severus	222–35
Maximinus Thrax	235–8
Gordian I and Gordian II	238
Pupienus and Balbinus	238
Gordian III	238–44
Philip the Arabian alone	244–7
Philip the Arabian and Philip	247–9
Decius	249–51
Treonianus Gallus and Volusianus	251–3
Aemilianus	253
Valerian and Gallienus	253–60
Gallienus alone	260–8
Claudius II (Gothicus)	268–70
Quintillus	270

Western Emperors

Eastern Emperors

Anastasius II and Artemius	713–15
Theodosius III	715–17
Leo III, the Isaurian	717–40
Constantine V and Copronymus	740–75
Leo IV the Khazar	775–9
Constantine VI	779–97
Irene	797–802

By the 8thC the Eastern Empire was the Byzantine Empire.

HOLY ROMAN (OR WESTERN) EMPERORS
Frankish Emperors

Charles (I) the Great (Charlemagne)	800–14
Louis (I) the Pious	814–40
Lothar I	840–55
Louis II (in Italy)	855–75
Charles (II) the Bald	875–7
Charles (III) the Fat	881–7
Guy of Spoleto (in Italy)	891–4
Lambert of Spoleto (in Italy)	894–8
Arnulf of Carinthia	896–901
Louis III of Provence	901–5
Berengar	905–24

Italian Emperors

Rudolf of Burgundy	924–6
Hugh of Provence	926–45
Lothar III	945–50
Berengar	950–62

German Emperors

Conrad I*	911–18
Henry I the Fowler*	918–36
Otto I the Great	936–73
Otto II	973–83

Otto III	983–1002
Henry II	1002–24
Conrad II	1024–39
Henry III the Black	1039–56
Henry IV	1056–1106
Henry V	1106–25
Lothar II	1125–37
Conrad III*	1138–52
Frederick (I) Barbarossa	1152–90
Henry VI	1190–7
Philip*	1198–1208
Otto IV	1198–1212
Frederick II	1212–50
Conrad IV*	1250–4

Interregnum
Competitors: Richard of Cornwall*, Alfonso of Castile*, Rudolf I of Hapsburg*, Adolf I of Nassau*, Albert I of Hapsburg*.

Henry VII of Luxembourg	1308–13
Louis IV of Bavaria	1314–47

Luxembourg Emperors

Charles IV	1347–78
Wenzel (or Wenceslas)*	1378–1400
Rupert of the Palatinate*	1400–10
Sigismund	1410–37

Hapsburg Emperors

Albert II of Hapsburg	1438–9
Frederick III (last emperor crowned in Rome)	1440–93
Maximilian I	1493–19
Charles V (last emperor crowned by Pope)	1519–56
Ferdinand I	1556–64
Maximilian II	1564–76
Rudolf II	1576–12

Matthias	1612–19
Ferdinand II	1619–37
Ferdinand III	1637–57
Leopold I	1658–1705
Joseph I	1705–11
Charles VI	1711–40
Charles VII of Bavaria	1742–5
Francis I of Lorraine	1745–65
Joseph II	1765–90
Leopold II	1790–2
Francis II	1792–1806

* Medieval emperors who were never crowned in Rome.

SOVEREIGNS OF THE BRITISH ISLES
Rulers of Scotland (from 1058)
House of Dunkeld

Malcolm III (Canmore)	1058–93
Donald Ban	1093–4
Duncan II	1094
Donald Ban *(restored)*	1094–7
Edgar	1097–07
Alexander I (the Fierce)	1107–24
David I (the Saint)	1124–53
Malcolm IV (the Maiden)	1153–65
William I (the Lion)	1165–1214
Alexander II	1214–49
Alexander III	1249–86
Margaret, Maid of Norway	1286–1290
John Balliol	1292–6
Robert I (the Bruce)	1306–29
David II	1329–71

House of Stuart

| Robert II | 1371–90 |

Robert III	1390–1406
James I	1406–37
James II	1437–60
James III	1460–88
James IV	1488–1513
James V	1513–42
Mary, Queen of Scots	1542–67
James VI *(ascended the throne of England 1603)*	1567–1625

Principal rulers of Wales (from 999)
DEHEUBARTH (Seisyllwg, Brycheiniog and Dyfed)

Llywelyn ap Seisyll	1018–23
Rhydderch ap Iestyn (usurper)	1023
Maredudd ab Edwin	1033–35
Hywel ab Edwin	1033, 1042–4
Gruffyd ap Llywelyn	1042–44
(King of Gwynedd & Powys from 1039)	
Gruffyd ap Llywelyn (second time)	1055–63
Maredudd ab Owain ab Edwin	c.1064
Rhys ab Owain	1072
Rhys ap Tewdwr	1078
Gruffydd ap Rhys	1135
Anarawd ap Gruffydd	1137–43
Cadell ap Gruffydd	1137–c.1151
Maredudd ap Gruffydd	c.1151–55
Rhys ap Gruffydd	c.1151–97

GWYNEDD

Cynan ap Hywel	999
Llywelyn ap Seisyll	1005
Iago ab Idwal ap Meurig	1023–39
Gwynedd & Powys annexed by	
Gruffudd ap Llywelyn, King of Deheubarth	1039
Bleddyn ap Cynfyn ap Gwerstan	1063
Trahaearn ap Caradog (twice)	1075

Gruffydd ap Cynan ap Iago	1075, 1081, c.1094
Owain Gwynedd	1137–70
Gwynedd divided between	
Cadwaladr ap Gruffydd and his sons	1170–1200

MORGANNWG (Glywysing and Gwent)

Rhys ab Owain ap Morgan	?
Hywel ab Owain ap Morgan	?
Meurig ap Hywel seized Gwent	c.1040
Cadwgan ap Meurig	c.1040–c.1055
Morgannwg taken by	
Llywelyn ap Iorwerth, King of Gwynedd	1055
Cadwgan ap Meurig (second time)	1063
Caradog ap Gruffydd ap Rhydderch	c.1073
Iestyn ap Gwrgant (usurper)	1081–c.1093
dispossessed by King William Rufus of England	

POWYS

Held by Gruffydd ap Llywelyn, King of Deheubarth	1039–63
Bleddyn ap Cynfyn ap Gwerstan/	
Rhiwallon ap Cynfyn (d. 1070)	1063
Madog ap Bleddyn/Rhirid ap Bleddyn	1075–88
Cadwgan ap Bleddyn	1075–1109
Madog ap Rhirid/Ithel ap Rhirid	1109–10
Territory frequently divided	1110–1200

By 1200 Welsh kings were lords owing allegiance to England and by 1282 Edward I had conquered Wales. His son was the first English Prince of Wales (b. Caernarvon, 25 April 1284).

Rulers of Ireland (from 1002)

Brian Boru *(King)*	1002–14
Donnchad *(King of Munster)*	1014–64
Toirdelbach *(King of Munster)*	1064–86

Muirchertach *(King of Munster)*	1086–1114
Toirdelbach More O'Connor *(High King)*	1119–53
Dermot MacMurrough *(King of Leinster)*	1134–71
Muirchertach MacLochlainn *(King)*	1153–66
Ruaidri O'Connor *(High King)*‡	1166–75

‡ The last native King of Ireland. The Pope granted Ireland to King Henry II of England in 1172.
Viking power in Ireland ended at the Battle of Clontarf in 1014. The 150 years of fighting which followed for the High Kingship contributed largely to the end of Irish royal rule.

Rulers of England (from 955) and of the United Kingdom (from 1801)
Saxon Line

Edwy	955–9
Edgar	959–75
Edward the Martyr	975–8
Ethelred the Unready	978–1016
Edmund Ironside	1016

Danish Line

Canute (Cnut)	1016–35
Harold I	1035–40
Hardicanute (Harthacnut)	1040–2

Saxon Line

Edward the Confessor	1042–66
Harold II (Godwinson)	1066

House of Normandy

William I (The Conqueror)	1066–87
William II	1087–1100
Henry I	1100–35
Stephen	1135–54

House of Plantagenet

Henry II (Curtmantel)	1154–89
Richard (The Lionheart)	1189–99
John (Lackland)	1199–1216
Henry III	1216–72
Edward I (Hammer of the Scots)	1272–1307
Edward II	1307–27
Edward III	1327–77
Richard II	1377–99

House of Lancaster

Henry IV	1399–1413
Henry V	1413–22
Henry VI	1422–61

House of York

Edward IV	1461–83
Edward V	1483
Richard III (Crookback)	1483–5

House of Tudor

Henry VII	1485–1509
Henry VIII	1509–47
Edward VI	1547–53
Jane (The Nine Days' Queen)	1553
Mary I (Bloody Mary)	1553–8
Elizabeth I (The Virgin Queen)	1558–1603

House of Stuart

James I of England and VI of Scotland	1603–25
Charles I	1625–49

Commonwealth (declared 1649)

Oliver Cromwell, Lord Protector	1653–8
Richard Cromwell	1658–9

House of Stuart

Charles II	1660–85
James II of England and VII of Scotland	1685–8
William III and Mary II (Mary d. 1694)	1689–1702
Anne	1702–14

House of Hanover

George I	1714–27
George II	1727–60
George III (Farmer George)	1760–1820
George IV (Prinny)	1820–30
William IV (Silly Billy)	1830–7
Victoria	1837–1901

House of Saxe-Coburg-Gotha (later Windsor)

Edward VII	1901–10

House of Windsor

George V (The Sailor King)	1910–36
Edward VIII (Our Smiling Prince)	1936
George VI	1936–52
Elizabeth II	1952–

SOVEREIGNS OF BELGIUM (FROM 1831)

Leopold I	1831–65
Leopold II	1865–1909
Albert I	1909–34
Leopold III	1934–51
Baudouin	1951–93
Albert II	1993–

Belgium became an independent kingdom in 1830.

SOVEREIGNS OF DENMARK (FROM 950)

Harold Bluetooth	950–85

Sweyn I (Forkbeard)	950–1014
Harold	1014–18
Canute the Great	1019–35
Canute III	1035–42
Magnus the Good	1042–7
Sweyn II Estrithson	1047–74
Harold Hen	1074–80
Canute IV (the Holy)	1080–6
Olaf I (Hunger)	1086–95
Eric I (Evergood)	1095–1103
Niels	1104–34
Eric II Emune (The Memorable)	1134–7
Eric III	1137–46
Sweyn III	1146–57
Knud III Magnussen	1157
Valdemar I (The Great)	1157–82
Canute VI	1182–1202
Valdemar II (The Victorious)	1202–41
Eric IV (Ploughpenny)	1241–50
Abel	1250–2
Christopher I	1252–9
Eric V	1259–86
Eric VI	1286–1319
Christopher II	1320–32
Valdemar	1340–75
Olaf II	1376–87
Margrethe I*	1387–1412
Eric VII	1412–39
Christopher III of Bavaria	1440–8
Christian I	1448–81
Hans	1481–1513
Christian II	1513–23
Frederick II	1559–88
Christian IV	1588–1648
Frederick III	1648–70

Christian V	1670–99
Frederick V	1746–1766
Christian VII	1766–1808
Frederick VI	1808–39
Christian VIII	1839–48
Frederick VII	1848–63
Christian IX	1863–1906
Frederick VIII	1906–12
Christian X	1912–47
Frederick IX	1947–72
Margrethe II	1972–

* Denmark, Sweden and Norway united under Queen Margrethe in 1397 (Union of Kalmar), making it the largest European monarchy of the time.

SOVEREIGNS OF MONACO (FROM 1427)

John I	1427–54
Catalan	1454–7
Claudine	1457
Lambert	1465
John II	1494–1505
Lucien	1505–23
Augustin	1523–32
Honoré I	1532–81
Charles II	1581–9
Hercules I	1589–1604
Honoré II	1604–62
Louis I	1662–1701
Antoine I	1701–31
Louise-Hippolyte	1731
James I	1731–3
Honoré III	1733–95
Honoré IV	1795–1819
Honoré V	1819–41

Florestan I	1841–56
Charles III	1856–89
Albert I	1889–1922
Louis II	1922–49
Rainier III	1949–

Monaco was annexed by France in 1793 and restored to the Grimaldi family in 1814.

SOVEREIGNS OF THE NETHERLANDS (FROM 1579)
The Dutch Republic
William I (The Silent), Prince of Orange*	1579–84
Maurice	1584–1625
Frederick Henry	1625–47
William II	1647–50
(*Position of Stadholder* suspended 1650–72)	
William III of Orange†	1672–1702
William IV	1747–51
William V‡	1751–95
Louis Bonaparte**	1806–10

Kingdom of the Netherlands
William I	1815–40
William II	1840–9
William III	1849–90
Wilhelmina	1890–1948
Juliana	1948–80
Beatrix	1980–

* Fought off Spanish rule to emerge as hereditary Stadholder.
† Succeeded to the British throne, 1688–9.
‡ Batavian Republic created by France in 1795.
** Napoleon established his younger brother as king. He abdicated in 1810 when Napoleon annexed Holland.

SOVEREIGNS OF NORWAY (FROM 1030)

Canute the Great	1030–5
Magnus the Good	1035–47
Harald Hardrade	1047–66
Olaf the Peaceful	1066–93
Magnus Barefoot	1093–1103
Eystein I	1103–22
Sigurd the Crusader	1103–35
Magnus the Blind (*rival king*)	1130–6
Inge I and Sigurd II	1136–61
Eystein II	1142–57
Haakon	1161–2
Magnus	1163–84
Sverre	1184–1202
Haakon III	1202–04
Inge Baardson	1204–17
Haakon IV	1217–63
Magnus the Lawmender	1263–80
Erik II	1280–99
Haakon V	1299–1319
Magnus VII	1319–55
Haakon VI	1355–80

SOVEREIGNS OF DENMARK AND NORWAY

Olav IV	1380–7
Margrethe	1387–1412
Erik of Pomerania	1389–1442
Christopher III of Bavaria	1442–8
Christian I	1448–81
John I	1481–1513
Christian II	1513–23
Frederick I	1559–88
Christian IV	1588–1648
Frederick III	1648–70

Christian V	1670–99
Frederick IV	1699–1730
Christian VI	1730–46
Frederick V	1746–66
Christian VII	1766–1808
Frederick VI	1808–14
Christian Frederick (Christian VIII of Denmark) (*Danish governor*)	1814

SOVEREIGNS OF SWEDEN AND NORWAY

Carl XIII	1814–18
Carl XIV*	1818–44
Oscar I	1844–59
Carl XV	1859–72
Oscar II†	1872–1905

* Carl XIV (Marshal Bernadotte) was originally one of Napoleon's generals. Elected as Crown Prince of Sweden, he fought with the allies against Napoleon in 1813.
† Abdicated in 1905 when Norway became independent.

SOVEREIGNS OF NORWAY (FROM 1905)

Haakon VII	1905–57
Olav V	1957–91
Harald V	1991–

SOVEREIGNS OF SWEDEN (FROM 1133)

Sverker	1133–56
Eric IX (*rival king*)	1150–60
Magnus Henriksson	1160–1
Carl VII	1161–7
Knut Eriksson	1167–95
Sverker Karlsson	1195–1208
Eric X	1208–16

John I Sverkersson	1216–22
Eric XI	1222–34
Knut Lange (*rival king*)	1229–34
Waldemar	1250–75
Magnus I Ladulas	1275–90
Birger II	1290–1318
(Union of Kalmar between Sweden and Norway, 1319)	
Magnus II Eriksson	1319–65
Eric XII (*co-regent*)	1356–9
Albert of Mecklenburg	1365–89
Margrethe (*regent*)	1389–1412
Eric XIII	1396–1439
(Union of Kalmar between Sweden, Norway and Denmark 1397)	
Engelbrekt Engelbrektsson	
(commander-in-chief)	1435–6
Karl Knutsson	1438–40
Christopher III of Bavaria	1440–8
Carl VIII (Karl Knutsson)	1448–57
Christian I of Denmark	1457–64
Carl VIII (Karl Knutsson)	1464–5
Jons Bengtsson Oxenstierna (*regent*)	1465–6
Erik Axelsson Tott (*regent*)	1466–7
Carl VIII (Karl Knutsson)	1467–70
Sten Sturethe Elder (*regent*)	1470–97
John II of Denmark (Hans)	1497–1501
Sten Sture (*regent*)	1501–3
Svante Nilsson Sture (*regent*)	1503–12
Sten Sture the Younger (*regent*)	1512–20
Christian II	1520–1
Gustavus Eriksson Vasa (*regent*)	1521–3
Gustavus I	1523–60
Eric XIV	1560–8
John III	1568–92
Sigismund	1592–9

Carl IX (*regent*)	1599–1604
Carl IX	1604–11
Gustavus II Adolphus	1611–32
Christina	1632–54
Carl X Gustavus	1654–60
Carl XI	1660–97
Carl XII	1697–1718
Ulrica Eleanora	1718–20
Frederick I of Hesse	1720–51
Adolphus Frederick	1751–71
Gustavus III	1771–92
Gustavus IV	1792–09
Carl (regent)	1792–6
Carl XIII	1809–18
(Sweden united with Norway 1814–1905)	
Carl XIV*	1818–44
Oscar I	1844–59
Carl XV	1859–72
Oscar II	1872–1907
Gustavus V	1907–50
Gustavus VI Adolf	1950–73
Carl Gustaf XVI	1973–

* Carl XIV (Marshal Bernadotte) was originally one of Napoleon's generals. Elected as Crown Prince of Sweden, he fought with the allies against Napoleon in 1813.

SOVEREIGNS OF SPAIN (FROM 1479)

Isabel I and Fernando V	1479–1504
Fernando (*regent*)	1505–6
Felipe I (The Handsome) (*regent*)	1506
Fernando (*regent*)	1507–16
Cardinal Cisneros (*regent*)	1516–17
Carlos I	1516–56
Felipe II	1556–98

Felipe III	1598–1621
Felipe IV	1621–65
Carlos II	1665–1700
Felipe V of Bourbon	1700–24
Luis I	1724
Felipe V	1724–46
Fernando VI	1746–59
Carlos III	1759–88
Carlos IV	1788–1808
José (Joseph) Bonaparte*	1808–13
Fernando VII	1808–33
Maria Cristina (*regent*)	1833–40
Don Baldomero Espartero (*regent*)	1840–3
Isabel II	1833–68
Francisco Serrano (*regent*)	1868–70
Amadeo of Savoy (*abdicated*)	1870–3
(First Republic	1873–4)
Alfonso XII	1874–85
Maria Cristina (*regent*)	1885–1902
Alfonso XIII (*dethroned*)	1886–31
(Second Republic	1931–75)
Juan Carlos I	1975–

* Imposed by Napoleon.

BRITISH PRIME MINISTERS

Monarch	Prime Minister	Party	Term of Office
George II	Sir Robert Walpole	Whig	1721–42
	Earl of Wilmington	Whig	1742–3
	Henry Pelham	Whig	1743–54
	Duke of Newcastle	Whig	1754–6
	Duke of Devonshire	Whig	1756–7
	Duke of Newcastle	Whig	1757–60
George III	Duke of Newcastle	Whig	1760–2

Monarch	Prime Minister	Party	Term of Office
	Earl of Bute	Tory	1762–3
	George Grenville	Whig	1763–5
	Marquis of Rockingham	Whig	1766
	Earl of Chatham	Tory	1766–8
	Duke of Grafton	Whig	1768–9
	Lord North	Tory	1770–82
	Marquis of Rockingham	Whig	1782
	Earl of Shelburne	Whig	1782–3
	Duke of Portland	Coalition	1783
	William Pitt	Tory	1783–1801
	Viscount Sidmouth	Tory	1801–4
	William Pitt	Tory	1804–6
	Lord Grenville	Whig	1806–7
	Duke of Portland	Tory	1807–9
	Spencer Perceval	Tory	1809–12
George IV	Earl of Liverpool	Tory	1812–27
	George Canning	Tory	1827
	Viscount Goderich	Tory	1827
	Duke of Wellington	Tory	1827–30
William IV	Earl Grey	Whig	1830–4
	Viscount Melbourne	Whig	1834
	Sir Robert Peel	Tory	1834–5
	Viscount Melbourne	Whig	1835–7
Victoria	Viscount Melbourne	Whig	1837–41
	Sir Robert Peel	Tory	1841–6
	Lord John Russell	Whig	1846–52
	Earl of Derby	Tory	1852
	Earl of Aberdeen	Peelite	1852–5
	Viscount Palmerston	Liberal	1855–8
	Earl of Derby	Tory	1858–9
	Viscount Palmerston	Liberal	1859–65

Monarch	Prime Minister	Party	Term of Office
	Lord John Russell	Liberal	1865–6
	Earl of Derby	Conservative	1866–8
	Benjamin Disraeli	Conservative	1868
	W E Gladstone	Liberal	1868–74
	Benjamin Disraeli	Conservative	1874–80
	W E Gladstone	Liberal	1880–5
	Marquis of Salisbury	Conservative	1885–6
	W E Gladstone	Liberal	1886
	Marquis of Salisbury	Conservative	1886–92
	W E Gladstone	Liberal	1892–4
	Earl of Rosebery	Liberal	1894–5
	Marquis of Salisbury	Conservative	1895–1901
Edward VII	Marquis of Salisbury	Conservative	1901–2
	A J Balfour	Conservative	1902–5
	Sir H Campbell-Bannerman	LIberal	1905–8
	H H Asquith	Liberal	1908–10
George V	H H Asquith	Liberal	1910–15
	H H Asquith	Coalition	1915–16
	D Lloyd George	Coalition	1916–22
	A Bonar Law	Conservative	1922–3
	S Baldwin	Conservative	1923–4
	J R Macdonald	Labour	1924
	S Baldwin	Conservative	1924–9
	J R Macdonald	Labour	1929–31
	J R Macdonald	National	1931–5
	S Baldwin	National	1935–6

Edward VIII (abdicated 1936)

George VI	S Baldwin	National	1936–7
	A N Chamberlain	National	1937–9
	A N Chamberlain	War Cabinet	1939–40

Monarch	Prime Minister	Party	Term of Office
	W S Churchill	War Cabinet	1940–5
	W S Churchill	Caretaker	1945
	C R Attlee	Labour	1945–51
	Sir W S Churchill	Conservative	1951–2
Elizabeth II	Sir W S Churchill	Conservative	1952–5
	Sir A Eden	Conservative	1955–7
	H Macmillan	Conservative	1957–63
	Sir A Douglas-Home	Conservative	1963–4
	H Wilson	Labour	1964–70
	E Heath	Conservative	1970–4
	H Wilson	Labour	1974–6
	J Callaghan	Labour	1976–9
	M Thatcher	Conservative	1979–90
	J Major	Conservative	1990–

US PRESIDENTS

President	Party	Term of Office
George Washington	Fed	1789–97
John Adams	Fed	1797–1801
Thomas Jefferson	Rep	1801–9
James Madison	Rep	1809–17
James Monroe	Rep	1817–25
John Quincy Adams	Rep	1825–9
Andrew Jackson	Dem	1829–37
Martin van Buren	Dem	1837–41
William H Harrison	Whig	1841
John Tyler	Whig	1841–5
James K Polk	Dem	1845–9
Zachary Taylor	Whig	1849–50
Millard Fillmore	Whig	1850–3
Franklin Pierce	Dem	1853–7

President	Party	Term of Office
James Buchanan	Dem	1857–61
Abraham Lincoln	Rep	1861–5
Andrew Johnson	Rep	1865–9
Ulysses S Grant	Rep	1869–77
Rutherford B Hayes	Rep	1877–81
James A Garfield	Rep	1881
Chester A Arthur	Rep	1881–5
Grover Cleveland	Dem	1885–9
Benjamin Harrison	Rep	1889–93
Grover Cleveland	Dem	1893–7
William McKinley	Rep	1897–1901
Theodore Roosevelt	Rep	1901–9
William Howard Taft	Rep	1909–13
Woodrow Wilson	Dem	1913–21
Warren G Harding	Rep	1921–3
Calvin Coolidge	Rep	1923–9
Herbert C Hoover	Rep	1929–33
Franklin D Roosevelt	Dem	1933–45
Harry S Truman	Dem	1945–53
Dwight D Eisenhower	Rep	1953–61
John F Kennedy	Dem	1961–3
Lyndon B Johnson	Dem	1963–9
Richard M Nixon	Rep	1969–74
Gerald R Ford	Rep	1974–7
James Carter	Dem	1977–81
Ronald Reagan	Rep	1981–9
George Bush	Rep	1989–93
William Jefferson Clinton	Dem	1993–

AUSTRALIAN PRIME MINISTERS

Name	Appointed
Rt Hon Edmund Barton	1901
Rt Hon Alfred Deakin	1903; 1905; 1909
Rt Hon J C Watson	1904
Rt Hon George Reid	1904
Rt Hon Andrew Fisher	1908; 1914
Rt Hon Joseph Cook	1913
Rt Hon W Hughes	1915
Rt Hon S M Bruce	1923
Rt Hon J H Scullin	1929
Rt Hon J A Lyons	1932
Rt Hon Sir Earle Page	1939
Rt Hon R W G Menzies	1939; 1949
Rt Hon A W Fadden	1941
Rt Hon John Curtin	1941
Rt Hon F M Forde	1945
Rt Hon J B Chifley	1945
Rt Hon Harold Edward Holt	1966
Rt Hon John G Gorton	1968
Rt Hon William McMahon	1971
Rt Hon E G Whitlam	1972
Rt Hon Malcolm Fraser	1975
Rt Hon R J L Hawke	1983
Rt Hon Paul Keating	1991

NEW ZEALAND PRIME MINISTERS

Name	Appointed
Rt Hon William Hall-Jones	1906
Rt Hon Sir Joseph George Ward	1906; 1928
Rt Hon Thomas MacKenzie	1912
Rt Hon William Ferguson Massey	1912; 1919
Rt Hon Sir Francis Henry Dillon Bell	1925
Rt Hon Joseph Gordon Coates	1925
Rt Hon George William Forbes	1930; 1931
Rt Hon Michael Joseph Savage	1935
Rt Hon Peter Fraser	1940
Rt Hon Sidney George Holland	1949
Rt Hon Sir Keith Jacka Holyoake	1957; 1960
Rt Hon Walter Nash	1957
Rt Hon John Ross Marshall (later Sir)	1972
Rt Hon Norman Eric Kirk	1973
Rt Hon Wallace Edward Rowling	1974
Rt Hon Sir Robert David Muldoon	1975
Rt Hon David Russell Lange	1984
Rt Hon Geoffrey Winston Russell Palmer	1989
Rt Hon J B Bolger	1990

Geography

BEAUFORT SCALE
The measurement of wind speed

Scale No.	Description	Speed mph (kph)	Characteristics on land
0	Calm	Less than 1 (1)	Smoke goes straight up
1	Light air	1-3 (1-5)	Smoke blows in wind
2	Light breeze	4-7 (6-12)	Wind felt on face; leaves rustle
3	Gentle breeze	8-12 (13-20)	Light flag flutters; leaves in constant motion
4	Moderate breeze	13-18 (21-29)	Dust and loose paper blown. Small branches move
5	Fresh breeze	19-24 (30-39)	Small trees sway
6	Strong breeze	25-31 (40-50)	Hard to use umbrellas. Whistling heard in telegraph wires
7	Moderate gale	32-38 (51-61)	Hard to walk into. Whole trees in motion
8	Fresh gale	39-46 (62-74)	Twigs break off trees
9	Strong gale	47-54 (75-87)	Chimney pots and slates lost
10	Whole gale	55-63 (88-102)	Trees uprooted. Considerable structural damage
11	Storm	64-75 (103-120)	Widespread damage
12-17	Hurricane	over 75 (120)	Violent, massive damage

Characteristics
at sea
Sea like a mirror

Ripples formed, but without foam crests

Small wavelets. Crests glassy but do not break

Large wavelets. Crests begin to break. Foam glassy, scattered white horses

Small waves. Fairly frequent white horses

Moderate waves. Many white horses. Chance of spray

Large waves, extensive white foam crests. Probably spray

Sea leaps up. White foam from breaking waves begins to be blown in streaks along wind direction

Moderately high waves. Edges of crests begin to break into the spindrift. Foam blown in well-marked streaks along wind direction

High waves. Dense streaks of foam along wind direction. Crests topple, tumble and roll over. Spray may affect visibility

Very high waves with long overhanging crests. Foam is blown in great patches along wind direction. Surface takes on a general white appearance. Visibility affected

Exceptionally high waves. Sea completely covered with long white patches of foam lying along wind direction. Visibility affected

Air is filled with foam and spray. Sea completely white with driving spray. Visibility seriously affected

RICHTER AND MERCALLI SCALES

The magnitude of earthquakes is measured in units on the Richter Scale and their intensity on the Mercalli Scale.

Mercalli	Richter	Characteristics
1	less than 3.5	Only detected by seismograph
2	3.5	Only noticed by people at rest
3	4.2	Similar to vibrations from HGV
4	4.5	Felt indoors; rocks parked cars
5	4.8	Generally felt; awakens sleepers
6	5.4	Trees sway; causes some damage
7	6.1	Causes general alarm; building walls crack
8	6.5	Walls collapse
9	6.9	Some houses collapse; cracks appear in ground
10	7.3	Buildings destroyed; rails buckle
11	8.1	Most buildings destroyed; landslides
12	greater than 8.1	Total destruction of area

SHIPPING AREAS

T	Tiree	**G**	Greenwich light vessel automatic ('Greenwich LV auto')
BL	Butt of Lewis	**C**	Channel
Su	Sumburgh	**Sc**	Scilly auto
F	Fifeness	**Va**	Valentia
Br	Bridlington	**R**	Ronaldsway
D	Dover	**M**	Malin Head
J	Jersey		

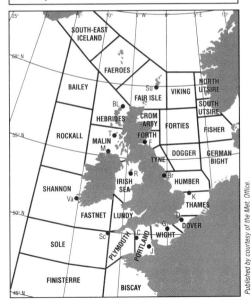

LARGEST CITIES

Name	Country	City Population (Census Year)	Rank	Urban Agglomeration (Census Year)	Rank
Seoul	South Korea	10,627,790 (1990)	1		
Bombay	India	9,909,547 (1991)	2	12,571,720 (1991)	7
São Paulo	Brazil	9,480,427 (1991)	3	15,199,423 (1991)	2
Moscow	Russia	8,801,500 (1991)	4		
Jakarta	Indonesia	8,254,000 (1990)	5		
Mexico City	Mexico	8,236,960 (1990)	6	14,987,051 (1990)	3
Tokyo	Japan	8,154,404 (1991)	7	11,718,720 (1989)	8
Shanghai	China	7,496,509 (1990)	8	12,670,000 (1989)	
New York	USA	7,322,564 (1990)	9	18,087,000 (1990)	1
Delhi	India	7,174,755 (1991)	10		
Los Angeles	USA			14,531,000 (1990)	4
Cairo	Egypt			14,000,000 (1990 estimate)	5
Calcutta	India			10,916,272 (1991)	9
Buenos Aires	Argentina			10,880,000 (1989)	10

LARGEST COUNTRIES

Name	Area (sq. km)
Russia	17,070,289
Canada	9,970,537
China	9,596,961
USA	9,155,579
Brazil	8,511,965
Australia	7,686,848
India	3,287,590
Argentina	2,766,889
Kazakhstan	2,716,626
Sudan	2,505,813

LARGEST DESERTS

Name	Continent	Area (000 sq. km)
Sahara	Africa	8,400
Australian	Australia	1,550
Arabian	Asia	1,300
Gobi	Asia	1,170
Kalahari	Africa	520
Turkestan	Asia	450
Takla Makan	Asia	320
Sonoran	N America	311
Namib	Africa	311
Thar	Asia	260

LARGEST ISLANDS

Name	Ocean	Area (sq. km)
Greenland	Arctic	2,175,600
New Guinea	Pacific	821,030
Borneo	Pacific	744,366
Madagascar	Indian	587,040
Baffin	Arctic	476,068
Sumatra	Indian	473,607
Honshu	Pacific	230,448
Great Britain	Atlantic	218,040
Ellesmere	Arctic	212,688
Victoria	Arctic	212,198

LARGEST LAKES

Name	Continent	Area (sq. km)
Superior	N America	82,100
Victoria	Africa	69,500
Huron	N America	59,570
Michigan	N America	57,750
Tanganyika	Africa	32,900
Baykal	Asia	31,500
Great Bear	N America	31,328
Malawi	Africa	28,880
Great Slave	N America	28,570
Erie	N America	25,670

HIGHEST MOUNTAINS

Name (all in Himalayas)	Height (m)
Everest	8,863
K2	8,607
Kangchenjunga	8,597
Lhotse	8,511
Yalung Kang	8,502
Makalu	8,481
Lhotse Shar	8,383
Dhaulagiri	8,167
Manaslu	8,156
Cho Oyo	8,153

HIGHEST WATERFALLS

Name	Country	Height (m)
Angel	Venezuela	979
Tugela	South Africa	947
Utigard	Norway	800
Mongefossen	Norway	774
Yosemite	USA	739
Ostre Mardola Foss	Norway	656
Tyssestrengane	Norway	646
Cuquenan	Venezuela	610
Sutherland	New Zealand	580
Kjellfossen	Norway	561

DEEPEST CAVES

Name	Country	Depth (m)
Reseau Jean Bernard	France	1,602
Shakta Pantjukhina	Georgia	1,508
Sistema del Trave	Spain	1,441
Aminakoateak	Spain	1,408
Snezhnaya	Georgia	1,370
Sistema Huautla	Mexico	1,353
Pierre St Martin	France	1,332
Boj-Bulok	Tajikistan	1,315
Sistema Cuicateca	Mexico	1,243
Reseau Rhododendrons– Gouffre Berger	France	1,242

LARGEST AND DEEPEST OCEANS

Name	Area (sq. km)	Greatest Depth (m)
Pacific	166,241,000	11,034
Atlantic	86,550,000	9,460
Indian	73,427,000	7,542
Arctic	13,223,700	5,450

LARGEST AND DEEPEST SEAS

Name	Area (sq. km)	Greatest Depth (m)
South China	2,974,600	6,505
Caribbean	2,753,000	7,239
Mediterranean	2,503,000	4,400
Bering	2,226,100	4,091
Gulf of Mexico	1,542,985	3,885
Sea of Okhotsk	1,527,570	3,400

LONGEST RIVERS

Name	Continent	Length (km)
Nile	Africa	6,670
Amazon	S America	6,448
Yangtze	Asia	6,300
Mississippi–Missouri	N America	6,020
Yenisey–Angara	Asia	5,540
Hwang Ho	Asia	5,464
Ob–Irtysh	Asia	5,410
Río de la Plata–Paraná	S America	4,880
Zaïre (Congo)	Africa	4,700
Lena–Kirenga	Asia	4,400

BUSIEST AIRPORTS

Name	Country	International Passengers (millions)
London Heathrow	UK	32.5
London Gatwick	UK	19.8
Frankfurt	Germany	19.5
Paris Charles De Gaulle	France	18.3
New York John F Kennedy	USA	17.9
Hong Kong Kai Tak	Hong Kong	16.2
Tokyo	Japan	16.1
Amsterdam Schiphol	Holland	15.3
Singapore Changi	Singapore	13.0
Zurich	Switzerland	11.0

LONGEST BRIDGES

Name	Country	Span (m)
Humber	UK	1,410
Verrazano Narrows	USA	1,298
Golden Gate	USA	1,280
Mackinac Straits	USA	1,158
Bosporus	Turkey	1,074
George Washington	USA	1,067
Ponte 25 Abril	Portugal	1,013
Forth Road	UK	1,006
Severn	UK	988
Quebec Rail	Canada	549

LONGEST CANALS

Name	Country	Length (km)
St Lawrence Seaway	Canada/USA	604.8
White Sea–Baltic	Russia	227
Göla	Sweden	185.1
Suez	Egypt	162
Volga–Moscow	Russia	128
Albert, Antwerp–Liège	Belgium	128
Volga–Don	Russia	100
Kiel	Germany	98
Houston	USA	91
Alphonse XIII	Spain	85

Religion

LARGEST RELIGIONS

Name	Worshippers (millions)
Christianity	1,784 (of which 1,101 are Roman Catholics)
Islam	951
Hinduism	655
Buddhism	310
Confucianism	200–300 (5.75 outside China)
Shintoism	3.2–35
Daoism (Taoism)	c.20
Judaism	18
Sikhism	16.5
Baha'i Faith	4.5

THE TEN COMMANDMENTS Exodus 20: 1–17
(*Good News Bible*)

God spoke, and these were his words: 2 'I am the Lord your God who brought you out of Egypt, where you were slaves.

3 'Worship no god but me.

4 'Do not make for yourselves images of anything in heaven or on earth or in the water under the earth.

5 Do not bow down to any idol or worship it, because I am the Lord your God and I tolerate no rivals. I bring punishment on those who hate me and on their descendants down to the third and fourth generation.

6 But I show my love to thousands of generations of those who love me and obey my laws.

7 'Do not use my name for evil purposes, for I, the Lord your God, will punish anyone who misuses my name.

8 'Observe the Sabbath and keep it holy.

9 You have six days in which to do your work,

10 But the seventh day is a day of rest dedicated to me. On that day

no one is to work – neither you, your children, your slaves, your animals, nor the foreigners who live in your country.

¹¹ In six days I, the Lord, made the earth, the sky, the sea, and everything in them, but on the seventh day I rested. That is why I, the Lord, blessed the Sabbath and made it holy.

¹² 'Respect your father and your mother, so that you may live a long time in the land that I am giving you.

¹³ 'Do not commit murder.

¹⁴ 'Do not commit adultery.

¹⁵ 'Do not steal.

¹⁶ 'Do not accuse anyone falsely.

¹⁷ 'Do not desire another man's house; do not desire his wife, his slaves, his cattle, his donkeys, or anything else that he owns.'

THE BEATITUDES Matthew 5:3-12
(*Good News Bible*)

³ 'Happy are those who know they are spiritually poor; the Kingdom of heaven belongs to them!

⁴ Happy are those who mourn; God will comfort them!

⁵ Happy are those who are humble; they will receive what God has promised!

⁶ Happy are those whose greatest desire is to do what God requires; God will satisfy them fully!

⁷ Happy are those who are merciful to others; God will be merciful to them!

⁸ Happy are the pure in heart; they will see God!

⁹ Happy are those who work for peace; God will call them his children!

¹⁰ Happy are those who are persecuted because they do what God requires; the Kingdom of heaven belongs to them!

¹¹ Happy are you when people insult you and persecute you and tell all kinds of evil lies against you because you are my followers.

¹² Be happy and glad, for a great reward is kept for you in heaven. This is how the prophets who lived before you were persecuted.

THE STATIONS OF THE CROSS
A devotional aid to meditation on the Passion of Christ.

1 Jesus is condemned to death.
2 Jesus bears his cross.
3 Jesus falls the first time.
4 Jesus meets his mother.
5 Jesus is helped by Simon.
6 Veronica wipes the face of Jesus.
7 Jesus falls a second time.
8 Jesus consoles the women of Jerusalem.
9 Jesus falls a third time.
10 Jesus is stripped of his garments.
11 Jesus is nailed to the cross.
12 Jesus dies on the cross.
13 Jesus is taken down from the cross.
14 Jesus is laid in the tomb.

THE TWELVE APOSTLES

Andrew	Peter (Simon)
James	John
Philip	Nathanael (Bartholomew)
Matthew (Levi)	Thomas
James (son of Alphaeus)	Judas (brother of James)
Judas Iscariot	Simon the Zealot

After the death of Judas Iscariot, the number was maintained at twelve by the election of Matthias.

THE FOUR LAST THINGS

Death	Judgement	Heaven	Hell

THE SEVEN SACRAMENTS

Baptism	Anointing of the Sick
Confirmation	Ordination
Eucharist	Matrimony
Penance	

THE SEVEN CHAMPIONS OF CHRISTENDOM

Name	Emblem
St George of England	Red cross on white ground
St Andrew of Scotland	Cross saltire gold on blue ground
St David of Wales	Dove
St Patrick of Ireland	Shamrock and snakes
St Denis of France	Carrying his severed head, witness to martyrdom
St James of Spain	Scallop shell
St Antony of Padua (Italy)	Lily, flowered cross and book

THE SEVEN FATHERS OF THE CHURCH

Early bishops and writers on doctrine.

St Athanasius	St Basil of Caesarea
St Gregory of Nazianzen	St Gregory of Nyssa
St John Chrysostom	St Cyril of Alexandria
St John of Damascus	

THE TWELVE TRIBES OF ISRAEL

Genesis 29–30, 35

The twelve tribes, by tradition, take their roots from the twelve sons of Jacob.

Reuben	Simeon	Levi
Judah	Dan	Naphtali
Gad	Asher	Issachar
Zebulun	Joseph	Benjamin

THE FOUR HORSEMEN OF THE APOCALYPSE
Revelation 6

Four riders whose arrival symbolizes the end of the world and the devastation and terror accompanying this event.

The rider of the White Horse carries a bow and wears a crown; he represents the Power of God triumphing over evil.

The rider of the fiery Red Horse carries a large sword and represents Bloodshed and War.

The rider of the Black Horse carries a pair of scales and represents Famine.

The rider of the Pale Horse is called Death and is closely followed by Hades; he represents Disease and Death.

THE TEN PLAGUES OF EGYPT Exodus 7–11

1 Water turns to blood
2 Frogs
3 Lice, sand flies or fleas
4 Swarms of flies
5 Cattle die from disease
6 Boils and sores
7 Hail
8 Locusts
9 Darkness
10 Death of first-born

THE SEVEN LAST PLAGUES Revelation 16

1 Sores
2 Sea turns to blood
3 Rivers turn to blood
4 People scorched by intense heat of sun
5 Darkness
6 River Euphrates dries up
7 Earthquake

THE SEVEN CORPORAL WORKS OF MERCY

Food to the Hungry
Clothing to the Naked
Visiting the Sick
Burying the Dead

Drink to the Thirsty
Harbouring the Stranger
Ministering to Prisoners

SAINTS AND SAINTS' DAYS

The list below shows a wide cross-section from the
many hundreds of saints who are, or were, venerated

JANUARY
1 Abbot Clarus
2 Basil, Gregory
3 Geneviève
4 Roger of Ellant
5 Simeon Stylites
6 Melanius
7 Raymond of Peñafort
8 Lucian, Nathalan
9 Adrian of Canterbury
10 Peter Orseolo
11 Alexander
12 Benedict Biscop
13 Bishop Hilary
14 Felix of Nola
15 Ita
16 Bernard and his
    Companions
17 Antony the Abbot
18 Prisca
19 Canute IV, King of
    Denmark
20 Sebastian, Fabian
21 Agnes
22 Vincent of Saragossa
23 Emerentiana
24 Francis de Sales
25 Dwyn
26 Paula
27 John Chrysostom
28 Thomas Aquinas
29 Gildas
30 Aidan
31 John Bosco

FEBRUARY
1 Brigid of Ireland
2 Joan de Lestonnac
3 Blaise
4 John de Britto,
    Gilbert of Sempringham
5 Agatha
6 Amand
7 Apollonia
8 Jerome Emiliani
9 Teilo
10 Scholastica
11 Finnian
12 Julian the Hospitaller,
    Seven Servite Founders
13 Huna
14 Valentine
15 Sigfrid
16 Juliana
17 Finan
18 Colman of Lindisfarne
19 Mesrop
20 Ulric of Haselbury
21 Peter Damian
22 Margaret of Cortona
23 Polycarp
24 Montanus and Lucius
25 Walburga
26 Porphyry of Gaza
27 Gabriel Possenti
28 Oswald

on the days shown. It is not intended to represent the calendar of any particular denomination.

MARCH
1 David
2 Chad
3 Cunegund
4 Adrian of Nicomedia
5 Bishop Ciaran
6 Baldred
7 Perpetua and Felicity
8 John of God
9 Dominic Savio,
  Frances of Rome
10 John Ogilvie
11 Eulogius of Cordoba
12 Pope Gregory the Great
13 Gerald of Mayo
14 Matilda
15 Louise de Marillac
16 Boniface of Ross
17 Joseph of Arimathea,
   Patrick
18 Fra Angelico,
   Cyril of Jerusalem
19 Joseph
20 Cuthbert
21 Abbot Benedict
22 Zachary
23 Turibius
24 Catherine of Sweden
25 Dismas
26 Ludger
27 Rupert of Salzburg
28 Guntramnus
29 Gwladys
30 John Climacus
31 Benjamin

APRIL
1 Hugh of Grenoble
2 Francis of Paola
3 Richard of Chichester
4 Benedict the Black
5 Vincent Ferrer
6 William of Eskill
7 John Baptist de la Salle
8 Walter of Pontoise
9 Waudru
10 Michael de Sanctis
11 Stanislaus
12 Pope Martin I
13 Guinoch
14 Tiburtius and Valerian
15 Ruadhan
16 Bernadette of Lourdes,
   Magnus of Orkney
17 Donnan
18 Apollonius the Apologist
19 Expeditus
20 Caedwalla, King of
   Wessex
21 Anselm
22 Theodore of Sykean
23 George
24 Ivo
25 Mark
26 Cletus
27 Zita
28 Peter Mary Chanel
29 Catherine of Siena
30 Adjutor

MAY

1 Peregrine Laziosi
2 Athanasius
3 Alexander and Eventius
4 Florian
5 Asaph
6 Adbert
7 John of Beverley
8 Victor Maurus
9 Pachomius
10 Cathal
11 Gengulf
12 Pancras
13 Andrew Fournet, Caradoc
14 Apostle Matthias
15 Dympna, Isidore the
   Farmer
16 Honoratus, John
   Nepomucen, Ubald
17 Paschal Baylon
18 Venantius, John I
19 Ivo of Kermartin,
   Pope Celestine V
20 Bernardino of Siena
21 Godric
22 Rita of Cascia
23 William of Rochester
24 David of Scotland
25 Venerable Bede,
   Gregory VII
26 Philip Neri
27 Augustine of Canterbury
28 Bernard of Montjoux
29 Bona
30 Ferdinand III of Castile
31 Petronilla

JUNE

1 Nicomede
2 Erasmus (Elmo)
3 Charles Lwanga
4 Petroc, Joan of Arc
5 Boniface
6 Norbert
7 Colman of Dromore
8 William of York
9 Columba of Iona
10 Landerious of Paris
11 Barnabas
12 Ternan
13 Antony of Padua
14 Basil the Great
15 Vitus
16 John Francis Regis
17 Alban
18 Mark and Marcellian
19 Romuald
20 Adalbert of Magdeburg,
   Mary, Our Lady of
   Consolation
21 Aloysius
22 John Fisher,
   Thomas More
23 Agrippina
24 John the Baptist
25 Febronia
26 Anthelm
27 Cyril of Alexandria,
   Kyned
28 Austell
29 Paul, Peter
30 Erentrude

JULY

1 Oliver Plunkett, Serf
2 Otto
3 Thomas the Apostle
4 Elizabeth of Portugal
5 Modwenna
6 Maria Goretti
7 Hedda of Winchester
8 Bishop Killian
9 Everildis, Virgin Mary, Queen of Peace
10 The Seven Brothers
11 Drostan
12 John Gualbert
13 Henry II
14 Camillus de Lellis
15 Swithin
16 Helier
17 Kenelm
18 Edburga of Winchester
19 Gervase, Protase
20 Margaret (Marina)
21 Laurence of Brindisi
22 Mary Magdalene
23 Apollinaris
24 Gleb, Christina
25 James the Great, Christopher, Margaret
26 Anne
27 The Seven Sleepers of Ephesus
28 Samson
29 Martha
30 Abdon, Sennen
31 Ignatius of Loyola

AUGUST

1 Alphonsus Liguori
2 Theodota of Nicaea
3 Germanus of Auxerre
4 John Mary Vianney
5 Afra
6 Justua, Pastor
7 Pope Sixtus II
8 Cyriacus, Dominic
9 Emygdius
10 Lawrence
11 Clare
12 Attracta
13 Hippolytus, Cassian of Imola
14 Athanasia of Aegina
15 Mary the Virgin
16 Roch, Stephen of Hungary
17 Hyacinth
18 Helen
19 John Eudes
20 Bernard of Clairvaux
21 Pope Pius X
22 Symphorian
23 Rose of Lima
24 Bartholomew
25 Louis of France, Genesius the Comedian
26 Ninian
27 Monica
28 Augustine of Hippo
29 Sebbi
30 Felix, Adauctus
31 Raymond Nonnatus, Aidan of Lindisfarne

SEPTEMBER

1 Fiacre, Giles
2 Brocard
3 Basilissa
4 Macnissi
5 Lawrence Giustiniani
6 Magnus of Fussen
7 Evurtius
8 Adrian, Natalia
9 Ciaran of Clonmacnoise
10 Nicholas of Tolentino
11 Deiniol
12 Guy of Anderlecht
13 Venerius
14 Notburga
15 Nicomedes
16 Cornelius, Ninian
17 Lambert
18 Joseph of Cupertino
19 Januarius
20 Eustace
21 Matthew
22 Maurice
23 Eunan, Adamnan
24 Gerard of Csanad
25 Finbarr
26 Cosmas and Damian, Cyprian
27 Vincent de Paul
28 Bernard of Feltre
29 Gabriel the Archangel, Michael the Archangel, Raphael the Archangel, Wenceslas
30 Jerome

OCTOBER

1 Remigius
2 Leger
3 Hewald the Dark and Hewald the Fair
4 Francis of Assisi
5 Maurus, Placid
6 Faith (Foi), Bruno
7 Osith
8 Pelagia the Penitent
9 Denis, Bishop of Paris, John Leonardi
10 Paulinus of York
11 Canice (Kenneth)
12 Ethelburga of Barking
13 Edward the Confessor
14 Callistus I
15 Teresa of Avila
16 Gall, Margaret Mary
17 Ignatius of Antioch, Etheldreda (Audrey)
18 Luke
19 Paul of the Cross
20 Andrew of Crete
21 Fintan Munnu
22 Donatus of Fiesole
23 John Capistrano
24 Antony Claret
25 Crispin and Crispinian, Marnock, Margaret Clitherow
26 Eata
27 Frumentius
28 Simon, Jude
29 Colman of Kilmacduagh
30 Marcellus the Centurion
31 Bega (Bee)

NOVEMBER

1 All Saints' Day
2 Marcian (Cyrrhus)
3 Pirminus, Martin de Porres, Hubert
4 Charles Borromeo
5 Zachary, Elizabeth
6 Leonard of Noblac, Winnoc
7 Willibrord
8 Four Crowned Martyrs
9 Benignus (Benen)
10 Leo the Great, Andrew Avellino
11 Martin of Tours
12 Josaphat
13 Britius, Homobonus, Francis Xavier Cabrini
14 Lawrence O'Toole
15 Albert the Great, Fintan of Rheinau
16 Margaret of Scotland
17 Hugh of Lincoln, Gregory the Wonderworker
18 Mawes
19 Nerses I
20 Edmund
21 Albert of Louvain
22 Cecilia
23 Clement I, Columban
24 Chrysogonus
25 Catherine of Alexandria
26 John Berchmans
27 Maximus, Catherine Laboure
28 James of the March
29 Saturninus
30 Andrew

DECEMBER

1 Eligius (Eloi)
2 Chromatius
3 Francis Xavier
4 Barbara, John Damascene
5 Birinus, Crispina
6 Nicholas of Bari
7 Ambrose
8 Budoc
9 Peter Fourier
10 Eulalia
11 Damasus, Corentin, Gentian
12 Jane Frances de Chantal
13 Lucy
14 John of the Cross
15 Mary di Rosa
16 Adelaide
17 Begga
18 Flannan
19 Anastasius I
20 Dominic of Silos
21 Peter Canisius
22 Chaeremon
23 John of Kanty, Thorlac
24 Delphinus
25 Anastasia, Eugenia
26 Stephen
27 John the Divine
28 The Holy Innocents
29 Thomas à Becket
30 Egwin
31 Sylvester

PATRON SAINTS OF THE UNITED KINGDOM

1 March	David of Wales
17 March	Patrick of Ireland
23 April	George of England
30 November	Andrew of Scotland

PATRON SAINTS AND INTERCESSORS

Profession, etc.	Saint	Date
Accountants	Matthew	21 September
Actors	Genesius the Comedian	25 August
Advertisers, advertising	Bernardino of Siena	20 May
Air stewards	Bona	29 May
Animals, sick	Nicholas of Tolentino	10 September
Animals, domestic	Antony the Abbot	17 January
Animals, danger from	Vitus	15 June
Apprentices	John Bosco	31 January
Archaeologists	Damasus	11 December
Archers	Sebastian	30 January
Architects	Thomas the Apostle	3 July
Armies, soldiers	Maurice	22 September
Artists	Luke	18 October
Astronauts	Joseph of Cupertino	18 September
Astronomers	Dominic	8 August
Asylums, mental	Dympna	15 May
Babies	Maximus	27 November
Bakers	Honoratus	16 May
Bankers	Matthew	21 September
Barbers	Cosmas and Damian	26 September
Bee-keepers	Bernard of Clairvaux	20 August
Birds	Gall	16 October
Blacksmiths	Eligius (Eloi)	1 December
Blind people	Thomas the Apostle	3 July
Book-keepers	Matthew	21 September
Booksellers, book trade	John of God	8 March
Boys, young	Dominic Savio	9 March

Profession, etc.	Saint	Date
Breast-feeding	Basilissa	3 September
Brewers	Amand	6 February
Bricklayers	Stephen	26 December
Brides	Nicholas of Bari	6 December
Bridges	John Nepomucen	16 May
Broadcasters	Gabriel the Archangel	29 September
Builders	Thomas the Apostle	3 July
Business people	Homobonus	13 November
Butchers	Luke	18 October
Cabinet makers	Joseph	19 March
Cake makers	Honoratus	16 May
Cancer sufferers	Peregrine Laziosi	1 May
Cemetery caretakers	Joseph of Arimathea	17 March
Charitable societies	Vincent de Paul	27 September
Chemists (pharmacists)	Cosmas and Damian	26 September
Childbirth	Raymond Nonnatus	31 August
Childless women	Anne	26 July
Children	Nicholas of Bari	6 December
Children, desire for	Rita of Cascia	22 May
Children, illegitimate	John Francis Regis	16 June
Christian people, young	Aloysius	21 June
Clergy	Gabriell Possenti	27 February
Clothworkers	Homobonus	13 November
Coffin-bearers	Joseph of Arimathea	17 March
Colic	Erasmus (Elmo)	2 June
Colleges	Thomas Aquinas	28 January
Comedians	Vitus	15 June
Construction workers	Thomas the Apostle	3 July
Contagious diseases	Roch	16 August
Cooks	Lawrence	10 August
Craftsmen and -women	Eligius (Eloi)	1 December
Criminals, condemned	Dismas	25 March
Crops, protection of	Magnus of Fussen	6 September
Customs officers	Matthew	21 September

Profession, etc.	Saint	Date
Dancers	Vitus	15 June
Deaf people	Francis de Sales	24 January
Death	Michael the Archangel	29 September
Death, happy	Joseph	19 March
Death, sudden	Andrew Avellino	10 November
Degree candidates	Joseph of Cupertino	18 September
Dentists	Apollonia	7 February
Devils, possession by	Cyriacus	8 August
Difficult situations	Eustace	20 September
Diplomatic services	Gabriel the Archangel	29 September
Disabled, physically	Giles	1 September
Disasters	Geneviève	3 January
Diseases, eye	Raphael the Archangel	29 September
Diseases, nervous	Dympna	15 May
Doctors	Luke	18 October
Dog bites	Ubald	16 May
Doubters	Joseph	19 March
Drought	Geneviève	3 January
Drowning, death by or danger from	Adjutor	30 April
Dying, the	Benedict	21 March
Earthquakes	Emygdius	9 August
Ecologists, ecology	Francis of Assisi	4 October
Eczema	Antony the Abbot	17 January
Editors	John Bosco	31 January
Education	Martin de Porres	3 November
Embroiderers	Clare	11 August
Emigrants	Francis Xavier Cabrini	13 November
Engineers	Ferdinand III of Castile	30 May
Epilepsy	Dympna	15 May
Examination candidates	Joseph of Cupertino	18 September
Falsely accused people	Raymond Nonnatus	31 August
Farmers	Isidore the Farmer	15 May
Farm workers	Benedict	21 March

Profession, etc.	Saint	Date
Fathers	Joseph	19 March
Fever	Geneviève	3 January
Fire, danger from	Agatha	5 February
Fishermen	Peter	29 June
Flood	Gregory the Wonderworker	17 November
Florists and flower growers	Rose of Lima	23 August
Flying	Joseph of Cupertino	18 September
Foresters	John Gualbert	12 July
Garage workers	Eligius (Eloi)	1 December
Gardeners	Fiacre	1 September
Girls, teenage	Maria Goretti	6 July
Glaziers	Lucy	13 December
Goldsmiths	Eligius (Eloi)	1 December
Grave-diggers	Joseph of Arimathea	17 March
Grocers	Michael the Archangel	29 September
Haemorrhage	Lucy	13 December
Hairdressers	Cosmas and Damian	26 September
Harvests	Antony of Padua	13 June
Headaches	Denis, Bishop of Paris	9 October
Health inspectors	Raphael the Archangel	29 September
Hernia sufferers	Cathal	10 May
Hoarseness	Bernardino of Siena	20 May
Hopeless cases	Jude	28 October
Horses	Eligius (Eloi)	1 December
Horse-riders	Martin of Tours	11 November
Horticulturalists	Fiacre	1 September
Hospitals	John of God	8 March
Housewives	Martha	29 July
Infertility	Rita of Cascia	22 May
Innkeepers	Gentian	11 December
Insanity	Dympna	15 May
Invalids	Roch	16 August
Jewellers	Eligius (Eloi)	1 December

Profession, etc.	Saint	Date
Joiners	Joseph	19 March
Journalists	Francis de Sales	24 January
Journeys, safe	Christopher	25 July
Judges	Ivo of Kermartin	16 May
Justice, social	Martin de Porres	3 November
Juvenile offenders	Dominic Savio	9 March
Lame people	Giles	1 September
Lawyers	Raymond of Peñafort	7 January
Learning	Catherine of Alexandria	25 November
Librarians, libraries	Jerome	30 September
Lighthouse keepers	Venerius	13 September
Lightning, protection against	Magnus of Fussen	6 September
Lost articles	Antony of Padua	13 June
Lovers	Valentine	14 February
Magistrates	Ferdinand III of Castile	30 May
Mariners	Francis of Paola	2 April
Maritime pilots	Nicholas of Bari	6 December
Marriages, unhappy	Gengulf	11 May
Married women	Monica	27 August
Medical profession	Cosmas and Damian	26 September
Merchants	Homobonus	13 November
Metalworkers	Eligius (Eloi)	1 December
Midwives	Raymond Nonnatus	31 August
Migrants	Francis Xavier Cabrini	31 November
Miners	Barbara	4 December
Missions	Francis Xavier	3 December
Mothers	Monica	27 August
Motorcyclists	Mary, Our Lady of Castellazzo	Unfixed
Motorists	Frances of Rome	9 March
Mountaineers	Bernard of Montjoux	28 May
Music	Cecilia	22 November
Naval officers	Francis of Paola	2 April

Profession, etc.	Saint	Date
Navigators	Francis of Paola	2 April
Neighbourhood watch schemes	Sebastian	20 January
Nervous diseases	Vitus	15 June
Notaries	Luke	18 October
Nurses	Camillus de Lellis	14 July
Old people	Mary, Our Lady of Consolation	20 June
Painters (artists)	Fra Angelico	18 March
Paratroopers	Michael the Archangel	29 September
Parenthood	Rita of Cascia	22 May
Park keepers	John Gualbert	12 July
Pawnbrokers	Bernard of Feltre	28 September
People in authority	Ferdinand III of Castile	30 May
Pets	Antony the Abbot	17 January
Philatelists	Gabriel the Archangel	29 September
Philosophers, philosophy	Catherine of Alexandria	25 November
Pilgrims	Nicholas of Bari	6 December
Poets	Columba of Iona	9 June
Policemen and -women	Michael the Archangel	29 September
Poor people	Antony of Padua	13 June
Possession by devils	Cyriacus	8 August
Postal workers	Gabriel the Archangel	29 September
Preachers	John Chrysostom	27 January
Pregnant women	Margaret (Marina)	20 July
Priests	John Mary Vianney	4 August
Printers	John of God	8 March
Prison officers	Hippolytus	13 August
Prisoners	Leonard of Noblac	6 November
Procrastination (against)	Expeditus	19 April
Publishers	John the Divine	27 December
Quantity surveyors	Thomas the Apostle	3 July

Profession, etc.	Saint	Date
Radio	Gabriel the Archangel	29 September
Radiologists, radiotherapists	Michael the Archangel	29 September
Rain, excessive	Geneviève	3 January
Rheumatism sufferers	James the Great	25 July
Sailors	Erasmus (Elmo)	2 June
Scholars	Thomas Aquinas	28 January
Scientists	Albert the Great	15 November
Sculptors	Luke	18 October
Secretaries	Genesius the Comedian	25 August
Security forces	Michael the Archangel	29 September
Security guards	Matthew	21 September
Short-sightedness	Clarus	1 January
Shorthand writers, stenographers	Cassian of Imola	13 August
Sick people	John of God	8 March
Signals, military	Gabriel the Archangel	29 September
Silversmiths	Eligius (Eloi)	1 December
Singers	Cecilia	22 November
Skiers	Bernard of Montjoux	28 May
Skin diseases	Antony the Abbot	17 January
Slander	John Nepomucen	16 May
Sleepwalkers	Dympna	15 May
Snakebites	Pirminus	3 November
Social justice	Martin de Porres	3 November
Social workers	John Francis Regis	16 June
Soldiers	Martin of Tours	11 November
Souls in purgatory	Nicholas of Tolentino	10 September
Stomach pains	Erasmus (Elmo)	2 June
Stonemasons	Four Crowned Martyrs	8 November
Storms, protection against	Vitus	15 June
Students	Thomas Aquinas	28 January

Profession, etc.	Saint	Date
Students, female	Catherine of Alexandria	25 November
Students, young	John Berchmans	26 November
Swimmers	Adjutor	30 April
Tailors, dressmakers	Homobonus	13 November
Tax officials	Matthew	21 September
Taxi drivers	Fiacre	1 September
Teachers	John Baptist de la Salle	7 April
Telecommunications	Gabriel the Archangel	29 September
Television	Clare	11 August
Theatre	Genesius the Comedian	25 August
Theft, protection against	Dismas	25 March
Thieves, danger from	Leonard of Noblac	6 November
Throat infections	Blaise	3 February
Toothache	Apollonia	7 February
Tradesmen and -women	Homobonus	13 November
Travellers	Christopher	25 July
Undertakers	Dismas	25 March
Unmarried women	Nicholas of Bari	6 December
Urgent situations	Expeditus	19 April
Vermin, protection against	Magnus of Fussen	6 September
Veterinary surgeons	Eligius (Eloi)	1 December
Waiters, waitresses	Martha	29 July
War victims (non-combatants)	Mary, Queen of Peace	9 July
Water, danger from	Florian	4 May
Widows	Paula	26 January
Wine merchants, wine trade	Amand	6 February
Workers	Joseph	19 March
Writers	Francis de Sales	24 January
Young people	Raphael the Archangel	29 September

ICONOGRAPHICAL EMBLEMS

Alms – John of God, Matilda

Altar – Philip Neri

Anchor – Clement I, Nicholas of Bari, Rose of Lima

Angel – Roch

Animal skins – John the Baptist

Arrow – Giles, Edmund, Teresa of Avila

Arrows – Christina, Sebastian

Axe – Barnabas, Boniface, John the Baptist, Magnus of Fussen, Thomas the Apostle

Balls (3) – Nicholas of Bari

Banner – George, Maurice, Michael the Archangel

Basket of bread – Nicholas of Tolentino

Bees – Ambrose, Bernard of Clairvaux, Isidore the Farmer, John Chrysostom

Bell – Abbot Benedict, Antony the Abbot, Francis Xavier

Birds – Francis of Assisi

Boat – Nicholas of Bari, Peter, Simon, Vincent of Saragossa

Book – Antony of Padua, Augustine of Hippo, Bernard of Clairvaux, Boniface, Ignatius of Loyola, Luke, Mark, Paul, Samson

Books – Teresa of Avila

Boys (3) in a tub – Nicholas of Bari

Bread – Geneviève, Antony of Padua, Roch

Bread in basket – Agatha

Broom – Martha

Brush – Luke

Bull, chained – Sylvester

Bush – Abbot Benedict

Candle – Blaise, Brigid of Ireland, Geneviève

Cannon – Barbara

Captives – Vincent Ferrer

Cardinal's hat – Jerome, Vincent Ferrer

Carpenter's square – Joseph
Carrying heads of dead nephews – Sigfrid
Chalice – Barbara, Bruno, Josephat, Thomas Aquinas
Chasuble – Ignatius of Loyola, Philip Neri
Children – Vincent de Paul
Chrism – Bernardino of Siena
Christ child – Antony of Padua, Christopher
City – Rose of Lima
Cloak – Martin of Tours
Club – Gervase and Protase, James the Less, Jude
Cock – Peter, Vitus
Column – Philip
Comb, iron – Blaise
Companion (Tobit) – Gabriel the Archangel
Cord – Lucy
Cross – Brigid of Ireland, Catherine of Siena, Francis Xavier, John
  Berchmans, Patrick, Rita of Cascia, Samson, Simon
Crown – Josephat, Sebastian, Wenceslaus
Crown of thorns – John of God, Louis of France, Rose of Lima
Crozier – Abbot Benedict, Giles, Pope Gregory the Great
Cruets – Joseph of Arimathea
Crutch – Maurus
Cup, broken – Abbot Benedict

Dagger – Edward the Confessor, Wenceslaus
Deer – Francis of Assisi
Devil – Geneviève
Devil, winged – Juliana
Dog – Eustace, Hubert, Roch, Vitus
Dog with torch in mouth – Dominic
Door – Anne
Dove – Ambrose, David, John Chrysostom, Pope Gregory the Great,
  Samson, Thomas Aquinas

Dragon – George, Margaret (Marina), Martha, Michael the
   Archangel
Dragon, chained – Sylvester
Dragon at feet – Juliana

Eagle – John the Divine
Eucharist – Ignatius of Loyola
Eyes in dish – Lucy

Fish – Antony of Padua, Francis of Assisi, Gabriel the Archangel
Flame over head – Brigid of Ireland
Fountain – Boniface
Fox – Boniface

Girdle – Monica
Globe – Henry
Globe of fire – Martin of Tours, Michael the Archangel
Goose – Martin of Tours
Greyhound – Ferdinand III of Castile
Gridiron – Lawrence, Vincent of Saragossa

Hair – Patrick
Halberd – James the Less
Head held in hands – Denis of Paris
Head on platter – John the Baptist
Heads of dead nephews, carrying – Sigfrid
Heart – John of God, Teresa of Avila
Herd – Geneviève
Hermitage – Giles
Hind – Giles
Hive – Bernard of Clairvaux

Infant Jesus – Joseph
Intestines – Erasmus (Elmo)

Key – James the Great
Keys – Geneviève, Martha, Peter, Petronilla, Zita

Ladder – John Climacus
Ladle – Martha
Lamb – Agnes, Catherine of Alexandria, John the Baptist
Lance – Barnabas, Dominic of Silos, Jude, Matthew, Matthias,
     Maurice, Thomas the Apostle
Last – Crispin and Crispinian
Lily – Antony of Padua, Catherine of Siena, Dominic, Joseph,
     Peter Mary Chanel
Lion – Jerome
Lion, winged – Mark
Loaves of bread – Philip
Lute – Cecilia

Man, winged – Matthew
Millstone – Christina
Monstrance – Clare, Norbert, Paschal Baylon, Thomas Aquinas

Nails – Joseph of Arimathea, Louis of France
Necklace – Etheldreda (Audrey)
Net – Andrew

Oak – Boniface
Oil in phial – Remigius, Walburga

Phial – Cosmas and Damian, Philip Neri
Pig – Antony the Abbot
Pilgrim's staff and hat – James the Great
Pincers – Christina, Eligius (Eloi)
Plane – Joseph
Pulpit – Vincent Ferrer
Purse – Matilda, Matthew

Rain, shower of – Swithin
Raven – Abbot Benedict, Boniface
Ring – Catherine of Alexandria, Catherine of Siena, Edward the
    Confessor
Rod – Joseph
Rosary – Dominic, John Berchmans
Rose – Rita of Cascia

Saltire – Andrew
Saw – Simon
Scales – Athanasia of Aegina, Maurus, Michael the Archangel
Scourge – Boniface, Gervase and Protase
Scroll – Paul
Shamrock – Patrick
Shell – James the Great
Ship – Francis Xavier
Shoe – Crispin and Crispinian
Shower of rain – Swithin
Skull – Francis of Assisi
Snakes – Patrick
Spade – Fiacre, Maurus
Square rule – James the Less, Jude
Staff – Samson
Stag with cross on antlers – Eustace, Hubert
Stage, miniature – Hubert
Star – Dominic, Nicholas of Tolentino, Thomas Aquinas
Stigmata – Catherine of Siena, Francis of Assisi
Stone – Stephen
Stones – Barnabas
Sun inscribed 'IHS' – Bernardino of Siena
Surgical instruments – Cosmas and Damian
Swan – Hugh of Lincoln
Sword – Boniface, Catherine of Alexandria, Gervase and Protase,
    James the Great, Michael the Archangel, Paul

Tablet – Bernardino of Siena
Tears – Monica
Thorn – Rita of Cascia
Tiara – Pope Gregory the Great, Sylvester
Tongs – Agatha
Tongs holding tooth – Apollonia
Torrent – Christopher
Tower – Barbara
Tree – Christopher
Trumpet – Vincent Ferrer
Tub with 3 boys – Nicholas of Bari

Veil – Agatha

Wax – Blaise
Wheel – Catherine of Alexandria, Christina
Windlass – Erasmus (Elmo)
Winged man – Matthew
Wolf – Francis of Assisi

TYPES OF CROSS

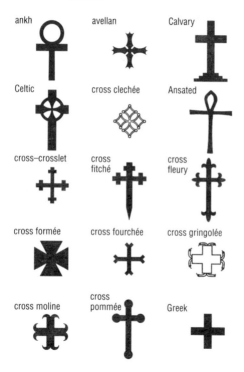

ankh

avellan

Calvary

Celtic

cross clechée

Ansated

cross–crosslet

cross fitché

cross fleury

cross formée

cross fourchée

cross gringolée

cross moline

cross pommée

Greek

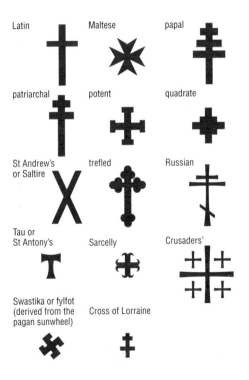

Latin

Maltese

papal

patriarchal

potent

quadrate

St Andrew's
or Saltire

trefled

Russian

Tau or
St Antony's

Sarcelly

Crusaders'

Swastika or fylfot
(derived from the
pagan sunwheel)

Cross of Lorraine

RELIGIOUS MONOGRAMS
The Chi–Ro or Sacred Monogram

'*Chi*' and '*rho*' are the first two letters of the Greek
word meaning 'Christ' and are represented by P and X.
The simple early forms slowly gave way to more
complex expressions.

Monograms based on Greek letters from the words 'Christ' or 'Jesus'

The Alpha and the Omega (Beginning and End)
These monograms combine the Greek *alpha* (*A*, *a*) and *omega* (Ω) with the cross and Chi–Ro monogram.

ECCLESIASTICAL SIGNS
Greek Cross
Used in some service books to indicate 'make the sign of the cross'. Also shown before the signatures of certain Church officials.

In Service Books

Response sign	Versicle sign	Denotes words to be intoned

POPES OF THE ROMAN CATHOLIC CHURCH
Note: This list does not include anti-popes.

c.42	Peter	189	Victor I
c.67	Linus	199	Zephyrinus
c.76	Anacletus	217	Calistus I
c.88	Clement I	222	Urban I
c.99	Evaristus	230	Pontian
c.107	Alexander I	235	Anterus
c.115	Sixtus I	236	Fabian
c.125	Telephorus	251	Cornelius
c.136	Hyginus	253	Lucius I
c.140	Pius I	254	Stephen I
c.155	Anicetus	257	Sixtus II
c.166	Soterus	259	Dionysius
175	Eleutherius	269	Felix I

275	Eutychian
283	Caius
296	Marcellinus
308	Marcellus I
310	Eusebius
311	Melchiades
314	Sylvester I
336	Mark
337	Julius I
352	Liberius
366	Damasus I
384	Siricius
399	Anastasius I
401	Innocent I
417	Zosimus
418	Boniface I
422	Celestine I
432	Sixtus III
440	Leo I (the Great)
461	Hilarius
468	Simplicius
483	Felix III (or II)
492	Gelasius I
496	Anastasius II
498	Symmachus
514	Hormisdas
523	John I
526	Felix IV
530	Boniface II
533	John II
535	Agapitus I
536	Silverius
537	Vigilius
556	Pelagius II
561	John III
574	Benedict I
578	Pelagius II
590	Gregory I (the Great)
604	Sabinian
607	Boniface III
608	Boniface IV
615	Deusdedit (Adeodatus I)
619	Boniface V
625	Honorius I
640	Severinus
640	John IV
642	Theodore I
649	Martin I
654	Eugenius I
657	Vitalian
672	Adeodatus II
676	Donus
678	Agatho
682	Leo II
684	Benedict II
685	John V
686	Conon
687	Sergius I
701	John VI
705	John VII
708	Sisinnius
708	Constantine
715	Gregory II
731	Gregory III
741	Zachary
752	Stephen II
752	Stephen III
757	Paul I
768	Stephen IV
772	Adrian I

795	Leo III	963	Leo VIII
816	Stephen V	964	Benedict V
817	Paschal I	965	John XIII
824	Eugenius II	973	Benedict VI
827	Valentine	974	Benedict VII
827	Gregory IV	983	John XIV
844	Sergius II	985	John XV
847	Leo IV	996	Gregory V
855	Benedict III	999	Sylvester II
858	Nicholas I	1003	John XVII
867	Adrian II	1004	John XVIII
872	John VIII	1009	Sergius IV
882	Marinus I	1012	Benedict VIII
884	Adrian III	1024	John XIX
885	Stephen VI	1032	Benedict IX
891	Formosus	1045	Gregory VI
896	Boniface VI	1046	Clement II
896	Stephen VII	1047	Benedict IX
897	Romanus	1048	Damasus II
897	Theodore II	1049	Leo IX
898	John IX	1055	Victor II
900	Benedict IV	1057	Stephen X
903	Leo V	1059	Nicholas II
904	Sergius III	1061	Alexander II
911	Anastasius III	1073	Gregory VII
913	Lando	1086	Victor III
914	John X	1088	Urban II
928	Leo VI	1099	Paschal II
928	Stephen VIII	1118	Gelasius II
931	John XI	1119	Callistus II
936	Leo VII	1124	Honorius II
939	Stephen IX	1130	Innocent II
942	Marinus II	1143	Celestine II
946	Agapitus II	1144	Lucius II
955	John XII	1145	Eugenius III

1153	Anastasius IV
1154	Adrian IV*
1159	Alexander III
1181	Lucius III
1185	Urban III
1187	Gregory VIII
1187	Clement III
1191	Celestine III
1198	Innocent III
1216	Honorius III
1227	Gregory IX
1241	Celestine IV
1243	Innocent IV
1254	Alexander IV
1261	Urban IV
1265	Clement IV
1271	Gregory X
1276	Innocent V
1276	Adrian V
1276	John XXI†
1277	Nicholas III
1281	Martin IV
1285	Honorius IV
1288	Nicholas IV
1294	Celestine V
1294	Boniface VIII
1303	Benedict XI
1305	Clement V
1316	John XXII
1334	Benedict XII
1342	Clement VI
1352	Innocent VI
1362	Urban V
1370	Gregory XI
1378	Urban VI

1389	Boniface IX
1404	Innocent VII
1406	Gregory XII
1417	Martin V
1431	Eugenius IV
1447	Nicholas V
1455	Callistus III
1458	Pius II
1464	Paul II
1471	Sixtus IV
1484	Innocent VIII
1492	Alexander VI
1503	Pius III
1503	Julius II
1513	Leo X
1522	Adrian VI
1523	Clement VII
1534	Paul III
1550	Julius III
1555	Marcellus II
1555	Paul IV
1559	Pius IV
1566	Pius V
1572	Gregory XIII
1585	Sixtus V
1590	Urban VII
1590	Gregory XIV
1591	Innocent IX
1592	Clement VIII
1605	Leo XI
1605	Paul V
1621	Gregory XV
1623	Urban VIII
1644	Innocent X
1655	Alexander VII

1667	Clement IX	1823	Leo XII
1670	Clement X	1829	Pius VIII
1676	Innocent XI	1831	Gregory XVI
1689	Alexander VIII	1846	Pius IX
1691	Innocent XII	1878	Leo XIII
1700	Clement XI	1903	Pius X
1721	Innocent XIII	1914	Benedict XV
1724	Benedict XIII	1922	Pius XI
1730	Clement XII	1939	Pius XII
1740	Benedict XIV	1958	John XXIII
1758	Clement XIII	1963	Paul VI
1769	Clement XIV	1978	John Paul I
1775	Pius VI	1978	John Paul II
1800	Pius VII		

* Born Nicholas Breakspear in Abbot's Langley, Hertfordshire.
The only Englishman so far to have been made Pope.
† In fact only the twentieth John but somehow an error of
calculation had been made in the past.

ARCHBISHOPS OF CANTERBURY

597	Augustine	805	Wulfred
604	Laurentius	832	Feologild
619	Mellitus	833	Ceolnoth
624	Justus	870	Aethelred
627	Honorius	890	Plegmund
655	Deusdedit	914	Aethelhelm
668	Theodore	923	Wulfhelm
692	Boerhtweald	942	Oda
731	Tatwine	959	Aefsige
735	Nothelm	959	Beorhthelm
740	Cuthbeorht	960	Dunstan
761	Breguwine	c.988	Athelgar
765	Jaenbeorht	990	Siggeric Serio
793	Aethelheard	995	Aelfric

1005 Aelfheah	1452 John Kemp
1013 Lyfing	1454 Thomas Bourchier
1020 Aethelnoth	1486 John Morton
1038 Eadsige	1501 Henry Dean
1051 Robert of Jumièges	1503 William Warham
1052 Stigand	1533 Thomas Cranmer*
1070 Lanfranc	1556 Reginald Pole
1093 Anselm	1559 Matthew Parker
1114 Ralph d'Escures	1576 Edmund Grindal
1123 William de Corbeil	1583 John Whitgift
1139 Theobald	1604 Richard Bancroft
1162 Thomas à Becket	1611 George Abbot
1174 Richard (of Dover)	1633 William Laud
1185 Baldwin	1660 William Juxon
1193 Hubert Walter	1663 Gilbert Sheldon
1207 Stephen Langton	1678 William Sancroft
1229 Richard le Grant	1691 John Tillotson
1234 Edmund Rich	1695 Thomas Tenison
1245 Boniface of Savoy	1716 William Wake
1273 Robert Kilwardby	1737 John Potter
1279 John Pecham	1747 Thomas Herring
1294 Robert Winchelsey	1757 Matthew Hutton
1313 Walter Reynolds	1758 Thomas Secker
1328 Simon Mepeham	1768 Frederick Cornwallis
1333 John Stratford	1783 John Moore
1349 Thomas Bradwardine	1805 Charles Manners Sutton
1349 Simon Islip	1828 William Howley
1366 Simon Langham	1848 John Bird Sumner
1368 William Whittlesey	1862 Charles Thomas Longley
1375 Simon Sudbury	1868 Archibald Campbell Tait
1381 William Courtenay	1883 Edward White Benson
1396 Thomas Arundel	1896 Frederick Temple
1398 Roger Walden	1903 Randall Thomas Davidson
1414 Henry Chichele	1928 Cosmo Gordon Lang
1443 John Strafford	

1942	William Temple	1980	Robert Alexander
1945	Geoffrey Francis Fisher		Kennedy Runcie
1961	Arthur Michael Ramsey	1991	George Leonard Carey
1974	Frederick Donald Coggan		

* Supported Henry VIII in his claims to be supreme head of the Church of England, thus severing links with Rome. Condemned for heresy in Queen Mary's reign and burned at the stake in Oxford in 1556.

BOOKS OF THE BIBLE

PROTESTANT CANON	ROMAN CATHOLIC CANON
Old Testament	**Old Testament**
Genesis	Genesis
Exodus	Exodus
Leviticus	Leviticus
Numbers	Numbers
Deuteronomy	Deuteronomy
Joshua	Joshua (Josue)
Judges	Judges
Ruth	Ruth
1 Samuel	1 Samuel (1 Kings)
2 Samuel	2 Samuel (2 Kings)
1 Kings	1 Kings (3 Kings)
2 Kings	2 Kings (4 Kings)
1 Chronicles	1 Chronicles (1 Paralipomenon)
2 Chronicles	2 Chronicles (2 Paralipomenon)
Ezra	Ezra (1 Esdras)
Nehemiah	Nehemiah (2 Esdras)
	Tobit (Tobias)
	Judith
Esther	Esther
Job	Job
Psalms	Psalms

Old Testament cont.	**Old Testament cont.**
Proverbs	Proverbs
Ecclesiastes	Ecclesiastes
Song of Solomon	Song of Solomon (Canticle of Canticles)
	The Wisdom of Solomon (Wisdom)
	Sirach (Ecclesiasticus)
Isaiah	Isaiah
Jeremiah	Jeremiah
Lamentations	Lamentations
	Baruch
Ezekiel	Ezekiel (Ezechiel)
Daniel	Daniel
Hosea	Hosea (Osee)
Joel	Joel
Amos	Amos
Obadiah	Obadiah (Abdias)
Jonah	Jonah (Jonas)
Micah	Micah (Micheas)
Nahum	Nahum
Habakkuk	Habakkuk (Habacuc)
Zephaniah	Zephaniah (Sophonias)
Haggai	Haggai (Aggeus)
Zechariah	Zechariah (Zacharias)
Malachi	Malachi (Malachias)
	1 Maccabees (1 Machabees)
	2 Maccabees (2 Machabees)
New Testament	**New Testament**
Matthew	Matthew
Mark	Mark
Luke	Luke
John	John

New Testament cont.	**New Testament cont.**
The Acts of the Apostles	The Acts of the Apostles
Romans	Romans
1 Corinthians	1 Corinthians
2 Corinthians	2 Corinthians
Galatians	Galatians
Ephesians	Ephesians
Philippians	Philippians
Colossians	Colossians
1 Thessalonians	1 Thessalonians
2 Thessalonians	2 Thessalonians
1 Timothy	1 Timothy
2 Timothy	2 Timothy
Titus	Titus
Philemon	Philemon
Hebrews	Hebrews
James	James
1 Peter	1 Peter
2 Peter	2 Peter
1 John	1 John
2 John	2 John
3 John	3 John
Jude	Jude
Revelation	Revelation (Apocalypse)

Apocrypha	**Apocrypha**
The First Book of Esdras	1 (3) Esdras
The Second Book of Esdras	2 (4) Esdras
Tobit	Tobit
Judith	Judith
The Rest of the Chapters of the Book of Esther	Additions to Esther
The Wisdom of Solomon	The Wisdom of Solomon
Ecclesiasticus or the Wisdom of	Sirach

Apocrypha cont.
Jesus, Son of Sirach
Baruch
A Letter of Jeremiah
The Song of the Tree
Daniel and Susanna
Daniel, Bel and the Snake
The Prayer of Manasseh
The First Book of the Maccabees
The Second Book of the Maccabees

Apocrypha cont.
Baruch
The Letter of Jeremiah
The Prayer of Azariah and the Song of the Three Young Men
Susanna
Bel and the Dragon
The Prayer of Manasseh
1 Maccabees

2 Maccabees

JEWISH TEXTS

The Law (Pentateuch)
Genesis
Exodus
Leviticus
Numbers
Deuteronomy

The Prophets
Joshua
Judges
Samuel
Kings
Isaiah
Jeremiah
Ezekiel
Hosea
Joel
Amos
Obadiah
Jonah
Micah
Nahum
Habakkuk
Zephaniah
Haggai
Zechariah
Malachi

The Writings
Psalms
Proverbs
Job
Song of Solomon
Ruth
Lamentations
Ecclesiastes
Esther
Daniel
Ezra
Nehemiah
Chronicles

THE KORAN
Chapters of the Koran

1. Entitled, The Preface or Introduction
2. Entitled, The Cow
3. Entitled, The Family of Imran
4. Entitled, Women
5. Entitled, The Table
6. Entitled, Cattle
7. Entitled, Al Araf
8. Entitled, The Spoils
9. Entitled, The Declaration of Immunity
10. Entitled, Jonas
11. Entitled, Hud
12. Entitled, Joseph
13. Entitled, Thunder
14. Entitled, Abraham
15. Entitled, Al Hejr
16. Entitled, The Bee
17. Entitled, The Night Journey
18. Entitled, The Cave
19. Entitled, Mary
20. Entitled, T.H.
21. Entitled, The Prophets
22. Entitled, The Pilgrimage
23. Entitled, The True Believers
24. Entitled, Light
25. Entitled, Al Forkan
26. Entitled, The Poets
27. Entitled, The Ant
28. Entitled, The Story
29. Entitled, The Spider
30. Entitled, The Greeks
31. Entitled, Lokman
32. Entitled, Adoration
33. Entitled, The Confederates
34. Entitled, Saba
35. Entitled, The Creator
36. Entitled, Y.S.
37. Entitled, Those who Rank themselves in Order
38. Entitled, S.
39. Entitled, The Troops
40. Entitled, The True Believer
41. Entitled, Are Distinctly Explained
42. Entitled, Consultation
43. Entitled, The Ornaments of Gold
44. Entitled, Smoke
45. Entitled, The Kneeling
46. Entitled, Al Ahkaf
47. Entitled, Mohammed
48. Entitled, The Victory
49. Entitled, The Inner Apartments
50. Entitled, K.
51. Entitled, The Dispersing
52. Entitled, The Mountain
53. Entitled, The Star
54. Entitled, The Moon
55. Entitled, The Merciful
56. Entitled, The Inevitable
57. Entitled, Iron

HINDU TEXTS

Hinduism has no single volume representing its doctrines. Of the many sacred writings which go to make up its fundamental beliefs, the following are considered to be the most significant:

The Vedas:
Rig-Veda
Sama-Veda
Yajur-Veda
Atharva-Veda

The Puranas:
Ramayana
Mahabharata (including the Bhagavadgita)
The Manu Smriti (Code of Manu)

BUDDHIST (PALI) TEXTS

1 Canonical Literature
The Three Baskets of Tripitaka
Vinaya Pitaka – Basket of Discipline
Sutta Pitaka – Basket of Discourses
Abhidharma Pitaka – Basket of the Higher Dharma
Note: Additional scriptures have been added by the various Buddhist schools.

2 Non-canonical Literature
a **Chronicles**
Dipavamsa – 'Island Chronicle'
Mahavamsa – 'Great Chronicle'
Culavamsa – 'Little Chronicle'
Mahabodhivamsa – 'Chronicle of the Bodhi-Tree'
Thupavamsa – 'Chronicle of the Stupa'

Daathavamsa – 'Chronicle of the Sacred Relic' (i.e. the Buddha's tooth)

Sasanavamsa – 'Chronicle of the Religion'

b Commentaries on Canonical Texts

These are too numerous to list, but among the most important are those composed by Buddhaghosa on the Vinaya Pitaka, the Digha Nikaya and on the first book of the Abhidharma Pitaka.

c Compendiums or manuals of Buddhist life and philosophy based on Canonical Texts

Again, too numerous to list but works such as the Visuddhimagga, the Malindapanha and the Abhidhammatthasangaha are the most important.

PRINCIPAL GODS
GREEK

Name of Deity	Representing/symbolizing
Zeus	God of gods
Poseidon	The sea; father of rivers and fountains
Hades	The underworld; death
Apollo	The sun
Hermes	Messenger and herald of the gods
Ares	War
Hephaestus	Fire
Dionysus	Wine
Uranus	Heaven
Hera	Goddess of the heavens; patroness and protector of marriage
Demeter	Abundance of corn and fruit; agriculture
Hestia	Hearth and home
Artemis	Moon, hunting, chastity
Athene	Wisdom
Aphrodite	Love and beauty
Hebe	Youth
Gaea	Earth

ROMAN

Name of Deity	Representing/symbolizing
Jupiter	God of gods
Neptune	The sea
Pluto	The underworld; death
Apollo	The sun
Mercury	Messenger of the gods
Mars	War
Vulcan	Fire
Bacchus	Wine
Coelus	Heaven
Saturn	Abundance
Juno	Queen of the heavens; guardian of women
Ceres	Agriculture
Vesta	Hearth and home
Diana	Hunting; chastity
Minerva	Wisdom
Venus	Love; beauty
Terra	Earth

Note: Saturn's day = Saturday

NORSE

Name of Deity	Representing/symbolizing
Odin	Chief god; war, wisdom, poetry, prophecy, magic
Thor	Thunder
Balder	Sun
Hermod	Messenger of the gods
Tyr	War; athletic activities. A hero, the killer of Game, the Hellhound
Forseti	Guardian of justice
Bragi	Poetry, wisdom and eloquence; welcomed dead warriors to the underworld

Name of Deity	Representing/symbolizing
Heimdal	Light; guardian of the Bifrost, the rainbow bridge leading to Valhalla
Hodur	Blind son of Odin; god of night
Vidar	Forests; 'the silent god'
Uller	Hunting
Vali	Son of Odin
Thjazi	Winter
Holler	Death
Mimir	Custodian of the Fountain of Wisdom
Ymir	Frost giant
Kari	Son of Ymir; controls air, storms
Hler	Son of Ymir; controls the sea
Logi	Son of Ymir; controls fire
Aegir	Giant of the seashore
Frey	Fruitfulness; sender of sunshine and rain
Frigga	Earth, air, conjugal love
Fulla	Mother goddess
Sjofna	Love
Lofn	Reconciliation of separated lovers
Vara	Punishment of unfaithful lovers
Syn	One of Frigga's attendants
Gerda	The frozen earth
Freyja	Fertility, love
Jord	Earth
Saga	History
Iduna	Spring; guardian of the apples which rejuvenated the gods
Bil	Child-deity; associated with waning moon
Siguna	Truth
Nanna	Wife of Balder; possessor of magic ring
Gefjon	Protection of girls who died unmarried

Name of Deity	Representing/symbolizing
Snotra	Wisdom
Gna	Messenger of the goddesses
Hel	The dead
Eir	Healing
Ran	Storms and the sea; drew the drowned under the waves in her net

Note: Odin's day (Anglo-Saxon 'Woden') = Wednesday; Thor's day = Thursday; Freyja's day = Friday

Other Figures
The three Norns represent Fate: Urda represents the past, Verdandi the present and Skuld the future. The thirteen Valkyries rode through the air and over the sea to select those who were to die in battle and whose souls were then transported to Valhalla where they enjoyed a perfect and everlasting existence, feasting and recounting their deeds of valour.

The elves were tiny creatures who plagued or helped mankind according to whim. The dwarfs lived in the heart of the hills and were metalworkers and jewellers. The giants stole summer and brought winter in its place. One of these was Hresvelgr who produced winds and storms by moving his wings.

EGYPTIAN
Name of Deity	Representing/symbolizing
Osiris	Earth, sky; principle of good
Set	Darkness; principle of evil
Ra	Sun
Shu	Dry atmospheres
Tefnut	Waters above the heavens

Name of Deity	Representing/symbolizing
Keb	Earth, vegetation
Pthah	Artisan of the world (made sun, moon, earth); holds world in his hands
Horus	Light
Anubis	The dead; art of embalming
Thoth	Art of letters; registrar and recorder of the underworld
Apis	Beast-god in form of a bull
Khem	Generation and production
Ranno	Gardens
Serapis	Healing
Isis	Earth, moon; has limitless powers
Maut	Mother of gods; mistress of sky
Athor	Sky, rising and setting sun; love and beauty
Maat	Truth; law and order
Mu	Light
Nephthys	The dead; personification of dusk
Neith	Upper heaven or ether
Anouke	War
Babastis	Gentle rays of the sun
Sekhet	Burning heat of the sun
Sphinx	Wisdom; earth's abundance
Anquet	Fertilizing waters of the Nile
Nut	Childbirth; nursing

Science

THE HUMAN BODY

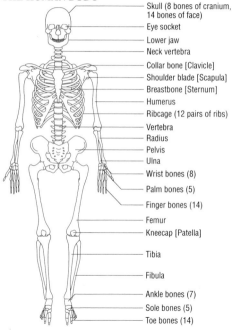

- Skull (8 bones of cranium, 14 bones of face)
- Eye socket
- Lower jaw
- Neck vertebra
- Collar bone [Clavicle]
- Shoulder blade [Scapula]
- Breastbone [Sternum]
- Humerus
- Ribcage (12 pairs of ribs)
- Vertebra
- Radius
- Pelvis
- Ulna
- Wrist bones (8)
- Palm bones (5)
- Finger bones (14)
- Femur
- Kneecap [Patella]
- Tibia
- Fibula
- Ankle bones (7)
- Sole bones (5)
- Toe bones (14)

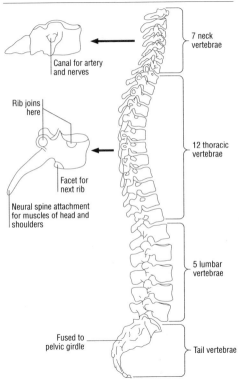

Canal for artery and nerves

7 neck vertebrae

Rib joins here

Facet for next rib

Neural spine attachment for muscles of head and shoulders

12 thoracic vertebrae

5 lumbar vertebrae

Fused to pelvic girdle

Tail vertebrae

GEOLOGICAL TABLE

Ages in millions of years (estimated)

Era	Period	Epoch	Time
Cenozoic	Quaternary	Holocene (recent)	c.0.01
		Pleistocene	c.2
	Tertiary	Pliocene	c.5
		Miocene	25
		Oligocene	40
		Eocene	55
		Palaeocene	65
Mesozoic	Cretaceous		135
	Jurassic		200
	Triassic		250
Palaeozoic	Permean		290
	Carboniferous		350
	Devonian		400
	Silurian		440
	Ordovician		500
	Cambrian		600
Precambrian	Proterozoic		2500
	Archaeozoic		3000
	Azoic		4000
			4500

Major Events	Animal and Plant Life
Ice Ages affect N Hemisphere temperature; sea retreats	End of Ice Age development of man; vegetation – Arctic forms to present form
Shallow seas in Europe	Mammals spread, early man
Thick unconsolidated clays	Whales and apes
Deposits on Great Plains	Modern mammals
Alpine-Himalayan mountain building.	First horses, elephants
	Early mammals
Chalk deposited in deep seas over Europe and Asia; marginal seas in N America	End of dinosaurs, flowering plants spread
Deep sea in Europe, swamps in N America	Giant dinosaurs, first birds
W Europe – shallow sea, red sands in N America	Small dinosaurs, first mammals
Shallow seas, continental deposits, mountain building	
Shallow seas over continents, extensive mountain building, coal formation	Forests formed coal, first reptiles
Erosion, large shallow seas, sandstones, thick shales	First forests and land animals, amphibians
Erosion, low areas resubmerged, mountain building in N America, Europe and Siberia	First land plants
Europe and N America mainly submerged; continental uplift	First fishes
Europe mainly submerged; N America submerged with large shallow areas	
	Sea animals without backbones, seaweeds
	First primitive plants and animals
	Earliest known rocks
	Earth formed

ELECTROMAGNETIC SPECTRUM

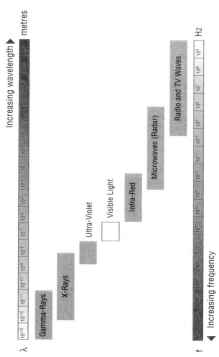

Increasing wavelength ▲

metres

Gamma-Rays

X-Rays

Ultra-Violet

Visible Light

Infra-Red

Microwaves (Radar)

Radio and TV Waves

Hz

λ

f

▼ Increasing frequency

CHEMICAL ELEMENTS

Name	Atomic Number	Symbol	Atomic Weight
Actinium	89	Ac	227.0278*
Aluminium	13	Al	26.98154
Americium	95	Am	243.0614*
Antimony	51	Sb	121.75
Argon	18	Ar	39.948
Arsenic	33	As	74.9216
Astatine	85	At	209.9870*
Barium	56	Ba	137.33
Berkelium	97	Bk	247.0703*
Beryllium	4	Be	9.01218
Bismuth	83	Bi	208.9804
Boron	5	B	10.81
Bromine	35	Br	79.904
Cadmium	48	Cd	112.41
Caesium	55	Cs	132.9054
Calcium	20	Ca	40.08
Californium	98	Cf	251.0796*
Carbon	6	C	12.011
Cerium	58	Ce	140.12
Chlorine	17	Cl	35.453
Chromium	24	Cr	51.996
Cobalt	27	Co	58.9332
Copper	29	Cu	63.546
Curium	96	Cm	247.703*
Dysprosium	66	Dy	162.5
Einsteinium	99	Es	254.0880*
Erbium	68	Er	167.26
Europium	63	Eu	151.96
Fermium	100	Fm	257.0951*
Fluorine	9	F	18.9984*
Francium	87	Fr	223.0197*
Gallium	31	Ga	69.72
Gadolinium	64	Gd	157.25
Germanium	32	Ge	72.59
Gold	79	Au	196.9665
Hafnium	72	Hf	178.49
Helium	2	He	4.0026
Holmium	67	Ho	164.9304

Name	Atomic Number	Symbol	Atomic Weight
Hydrogen	1	H	1.0079
Iodine	53	I	126.9045
Indium	49	In	114.82
Iridium	77	Ir	192.22
Iron	26	Fe	55.847
Krypton	36	Kr	83.8
Lanthanum	57	La	138.9055
Lawrencium	103	Lr	260.105*
Lead	82	Pb	207.19
Lithium	3	Li	6.941
Lutetium	71	Lu	174.97
Magnesium	12	Mg	24.305
Manganese	25	Mn	54.938
Mendelevium	101	Md	258.099*
Mercury	80	Hg	200.59
Molybdenum	42	Mo	95.94
Neodymium	60	Nd	144.24
Neon	10	Ne	20.179
Neptunium	93	Np	237.0482*
Nickel	28	Ni	58.71
Niobium	41	Nb	92.9064
Nitrogen	7	N	14.0067
Nobelium	102	No	259.101*
Oxygen	8	O	15.9994
Osmium	76	Os	190.2
Palladium	46	Pd	106.4
Phosphorus	15	P	30.97376
Platinum	78	Pt	195.09
Plutonium	94	Pu	244.0642*
Polonium	84	Po	208.9824*
Potassium	19	K	39.0983
Praseodymium	59	Pr	140.9077
Promethium	61	Pm	144.9128*
Protactinium	91	Pa	231.0359
Radium	88	Ra	226.0254*
Radon	86	Rn	222.0176*
Rhenium	75	Re	186.207
Rhodium	45	Rh	102.9055
Rubidium	37	Rb	85.4678

Name	Atomic Number	Symbol	Atomic Weight
Ruthenium	44	Ru	101.07
Samarium	62	Sm	150.35
Scandium	21	Sc	44.9559
Selenium	34	Se	78.96
Sodium	11	Na	22.98977
Silicon	14	Si	28.0855
Silver	47	Ag	107.868
Strontium	38	Sr	87.62
Sulphur	16	S	32.064
Tantalum	73	Ta	180.9479
Technetium	43	Tc	96.9064*
Tellurium	52	Te	127.6
Terbium	65	Tb	158.9254
Thallium	81	Tl	204.37
Thorium	90	Th	232.0381
Thulium	69	Tm	168.9342
Tin	50	Sn	118.69
Titanium	22	Ti	47.9
Tungsten	74	W	183.85
Unnilquadium	104	Unq	261.1087*
Unnilpentium	105	Unp	262.1138*
Unnilhexium	106	Unh	263.1182*
Unnilseptium	107	Uns	262.1229*
Unniloctium	108	Uno	265.1302*
Unnilennium	109	Une	266.1376*
Uranium	92	U	238.029*
Vanadium	23	V	50.9414
Xenon	54	Xe	131.3
Ytterbium	70	Yb	173.04
Yttrium	39	Y	88.9059
Zinc	30	Zn	65.381
Zirconium	40	Zr	91.22

* Indicates the atomic weight of the isotope with the longest known half-life.

PERIODIC TABLE

Calcium, gold and hydrogen are chemical elements which are examples of basic chemical substances. They cannot be broken down into simpler forms. This gives each element distinctive properties. The periodic table gives information about all the 103 known elements. (Elements 104 to 109 have been produced artificially but have not been officially named.)

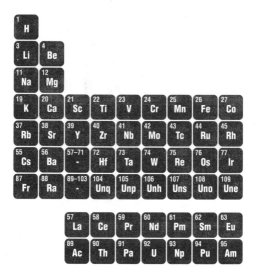

The periodic table was devised in 1869 by the Russian chemist Dmitri Mendeleyev. The table groups elements into seven lines or periods. As we read from left to right the elements become less metallic. The elements in each vertical group have similar chemical properties. Further information about the elements is given on pages 155–7.

MOHS' HARDNESS SCALE

This scale was invented by Friedrich Mohs (1773–1839), a German mineralogist, and is used for testing the hardness of materials by comparing them with the ten standard minerals.

Mineral	Simple hardness test	Mohs' Hardness
Talc	Crushed by fingernail	1.0
Gypsum	Scratched by fingernail	2.0
Calcite	Scratched by copper coin	3.0
Fluorspar	Scratched by glass	4.0
Apatite	Scratched by a penknife	5.0
Feldspar	Scratched by quartz	6.0
Quartz	Scratched by a steel file	7.0
Topaz	Scratched by corundum	8.0
Corundum	Scratched by a diamond	9.0
Diamond		10.0

GEMSTONES

Mineral	Colour	Mohs' Hardness
Agate	Brown, red, blue, green, yellow	7.0
Alexandrite	Green	7.5
Amethyst	Violet	7.0
Aquamarine	Sky blue, greenish blue	7.5
Beryl	Green, blue, pink	7.5
Bloodstone	Green with red spots	7.0
Carnelian	Red, reddish-yellow	7.0
Chalcedony	All colours	7.0
Chrysoprase	Apple green	7.0
Citrine	Yellow	7.0
Diamond	Colourless; tints of various colours	10.0

Mineral	Colour	Mohs' Hardness
Emerald	Green	7.5
Garnet	Red and other colours	6.5-7.25
Jade	Green, whitish, mauve, brown	7.0
Lapis lazuli	Deep blue	5.5
Malachite	Dark green banded	3.5
Moonstone	Whitish with blue shimmer	6.0
Onyx	Various colours with straight coloured bands	7.0
Opal	Black, white, orange-red, rainbow	6.0
Pearl	Pale greyish-white, black	–
Peridot	Pale green	–
Ruby	Red	9.0
Sapphire	Blue and other colours	9.0
Sardonyx	Reddish brown, white bands	7.0
Serpentine	Red and green	3.0
Soapstone	White, possibly marked by impurities	2.0
Sunstone	Whitish-reddish-brown with golden particles	6.0
Topaz	Blue, green, pink, yellow, colourless	8.0
Tourmaline	Brown-black, blue, pink, red, violet-red, yellow, green	7.5
Turquoise	Greenish-grey, sky blue	6.0
Zircon	All colours	7.5

SCIENTIFIC LAWS

Scientist	Dates	Type
Archimedes	287–212 BC	Principles
Avogadro, Amedeo	1776–1856	Hypothesis
Bernoulli, Daniel	1700–82	Principle
Blagden, Charles	1748-1820	Law
Boyle, Robert	1627–91	Law
Charles, Jacques	1746–1823	Law
Dalton, John	1766–1844	Law; Theory
Doppler, Christian	1803–53	Effect

Description

Principle of Displacement. When a body is totally or partially immersed in a fluid it experiences an upthrust equal to the weight of the fluid displaced.

Principle of Flotation. When a body floats it displaces a weight of fluid equal to its own weight.

Equal volumes of all gases at the same temperature contain the same quantity of molecules.

When the speed of a fluid increases the pressure in the fluid decreases, and when speed decreases pressure increases.

At constant pressure and for dilute solutions, the elevation of boiling point or the depression of freezing point of the solvent is directly proportional to the concentration of a given solute.

The volume of a given mass of gas is inversely proportional to its pressure, temperature remaining constant.

The volume of a given mass of gas is directly proportional to its absolute temperature, pressure remaining constant.

Law of Partial Pressures. In a mixture of gases, the pressure of a component gas is the same as if it alone occupied the space.

Atomic Theory. Elements are composed of atoms that can combine in definite proportions to form compounds.

The apparent change in frequency of sound or light caused by movement of a source with respect to the observer.

Scientist	Dates	Type
Einstein, Albert	1879–1955	Theory
Faraday, Michael	1791–1867	Laws
Gay-Lussac, Joseph Louis	1778–1850	Law
Graham, Thomas	1805–69	Law
Henry, William	1774–1836	Law
Hooke, Robert	1635–1703	Law
Le Chatelier, H L	1850–1936	Principle
Lenz, H F E	1804–65	Law

Description

Theory of Relativity. Mass and energy are related by the equation $E=mc^2$, where E is the energy produced by a mass change m, and c is the speed of light.

---

1. The mass of a given element liberated during electrolysis is directly proportional to the magnitude of the steady current used to the time for which the current passes.

2. The masses of different elements liberated by the same quantity of electricity are directly proportional to their chemical equivalents.

When gases react, they do so in volumes which bear a simple ratio to one another and to the volume of the product if it is a gas, temperature and pressure remaining constant.

Law of Diffusion. The rates of diffusion of gases are inversely proportional to the square roots of their densities.

The weight of gas dissolved by a liquid is proportional to the gas pressure.

The extension produced in a spring is proportional to the applied force.

If a system in chemical equilibrium is subjected to a disturbance it tends to change in a way which opposes the disturbance.

When a wire moves in a magnetic field, the electric current induced in the wire generates a magnetic field that tends to oppose the movement.

Scientist Newton, Sir Isaac	Dates 1642–1727	Type Laws
Ohm, Georg Simon	1787–1854	Law
Pascal, Blaise	1623–62	Law
Planck, Max	1858–1947	Theory
Pythagoras	580–500 BC	Theorem

PHYSICS – GASES

Scientist **Boyle, Robert**	Dates 1627–91

Description

Laws of Motion: 1. A body will continue in its state of rest or uniform velocity unless acted on by an unbalanced force.

2. The rate of change of momentum of a body varies directly to the force causing the change and takes place in the same direction as the force.

3. If a body A exerts a force F on a body B then B exerts a force -F on A; that is, action and reaction are equal and opposite.

4. If no external force acts on a system in a particular direction then the total momentum of the system in that direction remains unchanged.

Law of Gravitation. The force of the attraction between two given particles is inversely proportional to the square of their distance apart.

Voltage (V) in volts between ends of a conductor equals product of current (I) in amps flowing through it and its resistance (R): V=IR

In a fluid, pressure applied at any point is transmitted equally throughout it.

Quantum Theory: Light and other forms of energy are given off as separate packets (quanta) of energy.

In a right-angled triangle, the square on the longest side (the hypotenuse) is equal to the sum of the squares on the other two sides.

Description

The volume of a given mass of gas is inversely proportional to its pressure, temperature remaining constant.

Scientist	Dates
Charles, Jacques	1746–1823
Dalton, John	1766–1844
Henry, William	1774–1836
Avogadro, Amedeo	1776–1856
Gay-Lussac, Joseph Louis	1778–1850
Graham, Thomas	1805–69

PHYSICS – FLUIDS

Scientist	Dates
Archimedes	287–212 BC
Pascal, Blaise	1623–62

Description
The volume of a given mass of gas is directly proportional to its absolute temperature, pressure remaining constant.

Law of Partial Pressures. In a mixture of gases, the pressure of a component gas is the same as if it alone occupied the space. Atomic Theory. Elements are composed of atoms that can combine in definite proportions to form compounds.

The weight of gas dissolved by a liquid is proportional to the gas pressure.

Equal volumes of all gases at the same temperature contain the same quantity of molecules.

When gases react, they do so in volumes which bear a simple ratio to one another and to the volume of the product if it is a gas, temperature and pressure remaining constant.

The rates of diffusion of gases are inversely proportional to the square roots of their densities.

Description
Principle of Displacement. When a body is totally or partially immersed in a fluid it experiences an upthrust equal to the weight of the fluid displaced.
Principle of Flotation. When a body floats it displaces a weight of fluid equal to its own weight.

In a fluid, pressure applied at any point is transmitted equally throughout it.

Scientist	Dates
Bernoulli, Daniel	1700–82
Blagden, Charles	1748-1820

PHYSICS – ENERGY

Scientist	Dates
Hooke, Robert	1635–1703
Ohm, Georg Simon	1787–1854
Faraday, Michael	1791–1867
Doppler, Christian	1803–53
Lenz, H F E	1804–65
Planck, Max	1858–1947

Description
When the speed of a fluid increases the pressure in the fluid decreases, and when speed decreases pressure increases.

At constant pressure and for dilute solutions, the elevation of boiling point or the depression of freezing point of the solvent is directly proportional to the concentration of a given solute.

Description
The extension produced in a spring is proportional to the applied force.

Voltage (V) in volts between ends of a conductor equals product of current (I) in amps flowing through it and its resistance (R): V=IR

1. The mass of a given element liberated during electrolysis is directly proportional to the magnitude of the steady current used to the time for which the current passes.
2. The masses of different elements liberated by the same quantity of electricity are directly proportional to their chemical equivalents.

The apparent change in frequency of sound or light caused by movement of a source with respect to the observer.

When a wire moves in a magnetic field, the electric current induced in the wire generates a magnetic field that tends to oppose the movement.

Quantum Theory. Light and other forms of energy are given off as separate packets (quanta) of energy.

PHYSICS – RELATIVITY

Scientist	Dates
Einstein, Albert	1879–1955

PHYSICS – MOTION

Scientist	Dates
Newton, Sir Isaac	1642–1727

CHEMISTRY

Scientist	Dates
Le Chatelier, H L	1850–1936

MATHEMATICS

Scientist	Dates
Pythagoras	580–500 BC

Description
Theory of Relativity. Mass and energy are related by the equation $E = mc^2$, where E is the energy produced by a mass change m, and c is the speed of light.

Description
Laws of Motion: 1. A body will continue in its state of rest or uniform velocity unless acted on by an unbalanced force.
2. The rate of change of momentum of a body varies directly to the force causing the change and takes place in the same direction as the force.
3. If a body A exerts a force F on a body B then B exerts a force -F on A; that is, action and reaction are equal and opposite.
4. If no external force acts on a system in a particular direction then the total momentum of the system in that direction remains unchanged.
Law of Gravitation. The force of the attraction between two given particles is inversely proportional to the square of their distance apart.

Description
If a system in chemical equilibrium is subjected to a disturbance it tends to change in a way which opposes the disturbance.

Description
In a right-angled triangle, the square on the longest side (the hypotenuse) is equal to the sum of the squares on the other two sides.

INVENTIONS

Year	Invention/Discovery	Name and/or Country
c.3600-3500 BC	Writing	Sumerian civilization
2500 BC	Ink	China
1500 BC	Glassmaking	Mesopotamia
880 BC	Inflatable swimming aid	King Assur-Nasir Apli II of Assyria (to enable his troops to cross rivers)
650–600 BC	Coinage	Asia Minor
600 BC	Dictionary	Mesopotamia (written in Akkadian, a Babylonian/Assyrian language)
600 BC	City sewer	Cloaca Maxima, Rome, Italy
400 BC	Crossbow	China
400 BC	Kite	China
285 BC	Lighthouse	Pharos, near Alexandria
221 BC	Gunpowder	Alchemists, China
133 BC	Concrete	Used by Romans
100 AD	Writing paper	Cai Lun
180	Gimbals	China
180	Rotary fan	China
644	Windmill	Earliest recorded – Persia (Iran)
868	Printed book	*The Diamond Sutra*
1041	Printing (clay characters)	Bi Sheng
1250	Magnifying glass	Roger Bacon
1269	Compass	Petrus Peregrinus de Maricourt (some references say China c.1000/1100)
1281	Spectacles	Salvino degli Armati and his friend Alessandro della Spina

Year	Invention/Discovery	Name and/or Country
c.1381	Padlock	Inventor unknown
1447	Printing (moveable type)	Johannes Gensfleisch zur Laden zum Gutenberg
1498	Toothbrush	China
1520	Rifle barrel	August Kotter
1540	Pistol	Camillo Vettelli
1560	Camera obscura	Giovanni Battista della Porta
1589	Flush toilet	Sir John Harington
1590	Compound microscope	Hans and Zacharias Janssen
1608	Telescope	Hans Lippershey, perfected by Galileo Galilei in 1609
1638	Micrometer	William Gascoigne
1643	Barometer	Evangelista Torricelli
1644	Anemometer	Robert Hooke
1662	Spirit level	Jean de Melchisedech Thevenot
1672	Reflecting telescope	Isaac Newton
1680	Pressure cooker	Denis Papin, French assistant to Robert Boyle
1684	Thimble	Nicholas van Benschoten
1686	Meteorological map	Edmund Halley
1698	Steam pump	Thomas Savery
1711	Tuning fork	John Shore
1714	Mercury thermometer	Gabriel Fahrenheit
1718	Machine gun (flintlock)	James Puckle
c.1741	Centigrade scale	Anders Celsius
1752	Lightning conductor	Benjamin Franklin
1757	Sextant	Capt. John Campbell

Year	Invention/Discovery	Name and/or Country
1761	Scissors (en masse)	Robert Hinchcliffe
1762	Fire extinguisher	Dr Godfrey (some references say that it was not until 1816 that a Capt. George Manby invented it)
1768	Spinning Jenny	Thomas Higgs, perfected by James Hargreaves
1775	Tram	John Outram
1776	Submarine	David Bushnell
1783	Balloon	Joseph and Etienne Montgolfier
1787	Theodolite	Jesse Ramsden
1790	Wristwatch	Henri-Louis Jaquet Droz and Leschot
1797	Parachute	Andre Jacques Garnerin
c.1799	Electric battery	Alessandro Volta and Luigi Galvani
1804	Steam railway locomotive	Richard Trevithick
1807	Motorcar (gas)	Isaac de Rivez
1808	Typewriter	Pelegrino Turri
1815	Secateurs	Marquis Bertrand de Moleville
1816	Miner's safety lamp	Sir Humphry Davy
1816	Kaleidoscope	Dr David Brewster
1820	Soda water-making apparatus	Charles Cameron
1823	Talking doll	Johann Maelzel
1823	Waterproof rubber	Charles Macintosh
1826	Photography (metal)	Joseph Niepce
1828	Microphone	Prof. Charles Wheatstone (some references put this as late as 1925, perfected by the Bell Laboratories)

Year	Invention/Discovery	Name and/or Country
1828	Cocoa powder	Conraad Johannes van Houten
1830	Sewing machine	Barthelemy Thimonnier
1830	Electric telegraph	Samuel Morse
1831	Lawnmower	Edward Budding, for design; Ferrabee for manufacture
1835	Photography (paper)	William Fox Talbot
1835	Revolver	Samuel Colt
1839	Vulcanized rubber	Charles Goodyear
1839	Bicycle	Kirkpatrick Macmillan
1843	Christmas card	John Calcott Horsley
1847	Chloroform	Dr James Young Simpson
1849	Safety pin	Walter Hunt
1857	Toilet paper	Joseph Cayetty
1862	Milking machine	L O Colvin
1862	Refrigerator	James Harrison
1865	Tinned dog and cat food	James Spratt
1866	Dynamite	Alfred Nobel
1868	Stapler	Charles Henry Gould
1869	Margarine	Hippolyte Mege-Mouries
1869	Vacuum cleaner	Ives W McGaffey (some attribute this to Hubert Cecil Booth in 1901)
1871	Dynamo	Zenobe Gramme
1876	Telephone (articulating)	Alexander Graham Bell
1878–9	Light bulb	Edison and Swan Ltd
1879	Saccharine	Constantin Fahlberg
1879	Vaseline	Robert Cheseborough
1882	Electric iron	Henry W Seeley
1884	Fountain pen	Lewis Edson Waterman
1885	Spark plug	Etienne Lenoir

Year	Invention/Discovery	Name and/or Country
1885	Motorcar (petrol)	Gottlieb Daimler with Wilhelm Maybach, and Karl Friedrich Benz
1885	Motorcycle	Gottlieb Daimler
1886	Coca Cola	Dr John Pemberton (marketed as 'Esteemed brain tonic and intellectual beverage')
1887	Gramophone record	Emile Berliner
1887	Contact lens	Dr Eugen A Frick
1888	Pneumatic tyre	John Boyd Dunlop
1888	Roll-film for camera	George Eastman
1892	Escalator	Jesse W Reno and George H Wheeler
1893	Zip fastener	Whitcombe L Judson
1893	Kirby hairgrip	Hindes
1894	Flaked breakfast cereal	John and William Kellogg (Granose Flakes, renamed Corn Flakes four years later)
1895	X-rays	Wilhelm Konrad von Röntgen
1895	Motorcar (diesel)	Rudolf Diesel
1897	Radiator	Wilhelm Maybach
1899	Aspirin first marketed	Dr Felix Hoffman
1900	Paperclip	Johann Waaler
1900	Meccano	Frank Hornby
1901	Electric hearing aid	Miller Hutchinson
1902	Teddy bear	Simultaneously Morris Mitchan and Richard Steiff
1902	Disc brake	Dr Frederick Lanchester
1903	Car seat belt	Gustave Desire Liebau

Year	Invention/Discovery	Name and/or Country
1903	Aeroplane (first sustained flight)	Wilbur and Orville Wright
1904	Ovaltine	Dr George Wander
1906	Public broadcast (radio)	Reginald Aubrey Fessenden
1906	First practical rigid airship	Count Ferdinand Von Zeppelin
1907	Helicopter	Louis and Jacques Breguet
1907	Washing machine	Hurley Machine Co.
1908	Cellophane	Dr Jacques Edwin Branderburger
1909	Haircolour	Eugene Schueller
c.1910	Neon lighting	Georges Claude
1911	Nivea cream	Paul Beiersdorf
1912	Diesel locomotive	Sulzer Co.
1913	Crossword puzzle	Arthur Wynne
1913	Geiger counter	Ernest Rutherford and his assistant Hans Geiger
1919	Tea bags	Joseph Krieger
1920	Mars Bar	Frank Mars
1921	Insulin	Discovered by Paulesco
1922	Radar	A Taylor and L Young
1922	Choc-ice	C K Nelson
1924	Chanel No. 5	Coco Chanel
1924	Disposable handkerchiefs	Kimberley Clark Co.
1925	Scotch tape	Richard Drew, US (introduced into the UK from France as Sellotape)
1926	Aerosol can	Erik Rotheim
1926	Television	Baird, Scotland; Jenkins, US; Mihaly, Germany

Year	Invention/Discovery	Name and/or Country
1927	Pop-up toaster	Charles Strite
1928	Elastoplast	T J Smith and Nephew Ltd
1928	Penicillin	Alexander Fleming
1931	Metal detector	Gerhard Fisher
1933	Monopoly (board game)	Charles Darrow
1934	Perspex	Dr Rowland Hill
1935	Tape recorder	AEG GmbH
1937	Nylon	Dr Wallace Carruthers
1937	Instant coffee	Nestlé (first attempts took place in the US in 1867, with no great success)
1937	Jet engine	Frank Whittle
1938	Ballpoint pen	Laszlo and Georg Biro
1938	Domestic steam iron	Edmund Schreyer
1945	Tupperware	Earl W Tupper
1945	Atomic bomb	O Frisch, N. Bohr and R Peierls
1946	Bikini	Lousi Reard
1947	Transistor	William Shockley, John Bardeen and Walter Brattain
1948	Electronic computer	Frederick Williams
1948	Scrabble (board game)	James Brunot
1948	Velcro	George de Mestral
1950	Credit card	Ralph Schneider
1954	Non-stick pan	Marc Gregoire
1955	Lego	Ole and Godtfried Kirk Christiansen
1956	Contact lens (plastic corneal lens)	Norman Bier
1956	Oral contraceptive	Dr Gregory Pincus (first large-scale experimentation)
1956	Video recorder	Ampex Corporation

Year	Invention/Discovery	Name and/or Country
1957	Man-made earth satellite	*Sputnik*, USSR
1958	Cardiac pacemaker	Dr Ake Senning
1959	Hovercraft	Christopher Cockerell
1963	Fibre-tip pen	Japan Stationery Co. (known as Pentel)
1965	Word processor	IBM
1965	Miniskirt	Mary Quant
1971	Pocket calculator	Jack St Clair Kilby, James van Tassell and Jerry D Merryman
1971	Microprocessor	Intel Corp
1979	Rubik cube	Erno Rubik
1979	Compact disc	Sony, Japan with Philips, The Netherlands
1980	Halogen lamp	Philips
1981	Superchip	Hewlett-Packard
1981	Post-it Notes	Dr Spencer Sylver
1981	Trivial Pursuit (board game)	Chris and John Haney and Scott Abbott

The Arts

PRINCIPAL ART MOVEMENTS, ARTISTS, SCULPTORS AND ARCHITECTS IN WESTERN ART

These listings give a general guide to the major international art movements, and the artists, sculptors and architects who were active in those periods. The working lives of many of the artists spanned more than one stylistic change but, in order to avoid repetition, they are noted only once.

Period: 11thC and 12thC

Movement: Romanesque (known in Britain as **Norman**, the first European style to become internationally recognized)

Painters/artists: Names of individuals largely unknown; *examples include* paintings in churches at St Savin-sur-Gartempe; San Clemente (Rome). *Book illumination:* Winchester Bible. *Needlework:* Bayeux Tapestry.

Sculptors: Names of individuals largely unknown; *examples include* church sculpture at: Moissac, Autun (by Gislebertus); Vézelay; St Michael (Hildesheim); Novgorod; Guesen (Poland). *Secular examples include* the bronze lion in Brunswick.

Architects: Names of individuals largely unknown; *examples include* churches/cathedrals at: St Serznin (Toulouse); Jumièges; St Michael (Hildesheim); Limburg; Trier; Pisa; Winchester; Ely; Peterborough; Norwich; Durham. *Secular examples include* The Tower of London.

Period: mid-12thC–mid-16thC

Movements: Gothic (Gothic, High Gothic, Flamboyant Gothic, International Gothic)

Painters/artists: Giotto; Lorenzetti (Pietro and Ambrogio); Cimabue; Uccello. *Book illumination:* Queen Mary's Psalter; Très Riches

Heures (by Pol de Limburg and his brothers Herman and Jean); Aeneid (by Heinrich von Veldecke); Troy Romances (by Benois de St Moire). *Panel painting:* Duccio; Martini.

Sculptors: Ghiberti; Pisano (Nicola and Giovanni); Sluter.

Architects: Names of individuals largely unknown; *examples include* churches/cathedrals at: St Denis (near Paris); Noyon; Laon; Notre Dame (Paris); Canterbury (choir designed by William of Sens); Lincoln (nave); Chartres; Reims; Amiens; Cologne. *Cathedral towers at:* Ulm; Strasbourg. *Secular examples include:* Ca' d'Oro and Doge's Palace (Venice); New College (Oxford); Cloth Hall (Bruges).

Period: c.15thC–early 17thC
Movements: Renaissance (Early Renaissance, High Renaissance); Mannerism
Painters/artists: Altdorfer; Bellini; Botticelli; Bronzino; Bruegel; Burgkmair; Carracci; Castagno; Corregio; Cranach; Dürer; Elsheimer; Van Eyck; della Francesca; El Greco; Giorgione; Heemskerck; Hilliard; Holbein the Younger; Leonardo da Vinci; van Leyden; Mantegna; Masaccio; Massys; Michelangelo; Parmigiano; Raphael; van Scorel; Tintoretto; Titian; Veronese; van der Weyden.

Sculptors: Bertoldo; Cellini; Donatello; Giambologna; Goujon; Meit; Michelangelo; Pollaiuolo; Riccio; Torrigiano; Vischer; Vittoria.

Architects: Alberti; Bramante of Urbino; Brunelleschi; Campbell; Palladio; Romano.

Period: 17thC–early 18thC
Movement: Baroque
Painters/artists: Caravaggio; Cortona; van Dyck; Giordano; Hals; Jordaens; Kalf; Le Brun; Murillo; Poussin; Pozzo; Rembrandt; Rubens; Ruisdael; Thornhill; Velázquez.

Sculptors: Bernini; Bushnell; Gibbons; Montañés; Permoser; Puget; Quellin; Raggi.

Architects: Bernini; Borromini; Cortona; Fischer von Erlach; Guarini; Hawksmoor; Jones; Longhena; Maderna; Mansart; Vanbrugh; Wren.

Period: c. early–mid-18thC
Movement: Rococo
Painters/artists: Boucher; Canaletto; Chardin; Fragonard; Gainsborough; Guardi; Hogarth; Longhi; Tiepolo; Troy; Watteau.
Sculptors: Falconet; Günther.
Architects: Boffrand; Cotte; Cuvilliés; Gabriel; Le Pautre; Neumann; Pöppelmann; Zimmermann.

Period: c. late 18thC–early 19thC
Movements: Neoclassicism (influenced other styles such as **Louis XVI, Régence, Directoire and Empire** (in France); **Adam, Regency,** and **Hepplewhite and Sheraton furniture** (in Britain)).
Painters/artists: Barry; Copley; Dance; David; Goya; Hamilton; Ingres; Kauffmann; Raeburn; Reynolds; Vien; West.
Sculptors: Canova; Flaxman; Gibson; Houdon; Powers; Schadow; Stubbs; Thorvaldsen.
Architects: Adam brothers; Boullée; Chambers; Dance; Langhans; Ledoux; Nash; Soane; Soufflot; 'Greek' Thomson; Zakharov.

Period: c. late 18thC–late 19thC
Movements: Romanticism (influenced other styles such as **Gothic Revival, Greek Revival, Pre-Raphaelite, Arts and Crafts**); **Historicism; Realism.**
Painters/artists: Blake; Boudin; Cole; Constable; Corot; Courbet; Daumier; Delacroix; Delaroche; Eakins; Friedrich; Fuseli; Géricault; Homer; Hunt; Landseer; Manet; Millais; Millet; Morris; Rossetti; Ruskin; Turner.
Sculptors: Carpeaux; Daumier; Rodin; Rude; Stevens.
Architects: Barry; Paxton; Pugin; Schinkel; Shaw; Upjohn; Webb; Wyatt.

Period: c. mid-19thC–early 20thC
Movements: Impressionism; Neo-Impressionism; Symbolism; Post-Impressionism; Art Nouveau; Cubism; Fauvism; Expressionism; Futurism.

Painters/artists: Balla; Bazille; Beardsley; Bernard; Boccioni; Bonnard; Braque; Burne-Jones; Caillebotte; Carra; Cassatt; Cézanne; Chagall; Puvis de Chavannes; Cross; Degas; Delaunay; Dérain; Dix; Duchamp; Dufy; Ensor; Forain; La Fresnaye; Gauguin; Gleizes; Van Gogh; Gris; Grosz; von Jawlensky; Kokoschka; Klimt; Léger; Marc; Marquet; Matisse; Metzinger; Modigliani; Monet; Moreau; Morisot; Munch; Nolde; Picasso; Pissarro; Redon; Renoir; Rivera; Rouault; Seurat; Severini; Signac; Sisley; Soutine; Toulouse-Lautrec; Vlaminck; Vuillard.

Sculptors: Archipenko; Barlach; Bourdelle; Brancusi; Degas; Despiau; Dobson; Duchamp-Villon; Gaudier-Brzeska; González; Gris; Laurens; Lehmbruck; Lipchitz; Maillol; Rosso.

Architects: Behrens; Gaudi; Horta; Mackintosh; Sullivan; van der Velde; Voysey.

Period: c.1915–c.1950
Movements: Dadaism; De Stijl; Constructivism; Surrealism; Bauhaus; Art Deco
Painters/artists: Bacon; de' Chirico; Dali; Dobell; van Doesburg; Duchamp; Ernst; John; Kandinsky; Klee; Magritte; Miró; Moholy-Nagy; Mondrian; Morandi; Nicholson; Picabia; Ray; Schwitters; Tanguy.

Sculptors: Arp; Epstein; Gabo; Gill; Hepworth; Milles; Moore; Paolozzi; Pevsner; Tatlin; Vantongerloo.

Architects: Breuer; Le Corbusier; Garnier; Gropius; Lutyens; Mies van der Rohe; Perret; Wright.

Period: c.1940–present
Movements: Abstract Expressionism; Pop Art; Conceptual Art (including **Body, Performance, Land and Minimal Art**); **Photo-Realism; Post-Modernism**
Painters/artists: Auerbach; Baselitz; Beuys; Blake; Bratby; Buffet; Campbell; Caulfield; Chagall; Christo; Dine; Fontana; Freud; Gorky; Hockney; Johns; Jones; Kitaj; Kline; de Kooning; Kossoff; Lichtenstein; Lüpertz; Manzoni; Morley; Motherwell; Pollock;

Rauschenberg; Rivers; Rosenquist; Rothko; Schnabel; Stella; Tobey; Warhol.

Sculptors: Andre; Armitage; Beuys; Butter; Calder; Caro; Chadwick; Frink; Giacometti; Johns; Judd; King; Long; Marini; Morris; Oldenburg; Segal; Smith; Wotruba.

Architects: Aalto; Foster; Graves; Hertzberger; Jencks; Johnson; Kahn; Lasdun; Piano; Rogers; Rossi; Smithson; Stirling; Utzon.

PRINCIPAL MUSICAL MOVEMENTS AND COMPOSERS IN WESTERN MUSIC

Period: c.1320– c.1690
Movement: Renaissance
Composers: Bologna; Busnois; Byrd; Cabezón; Dufay; Dunstable; Frescobaldi; Gabrieli (A); Gibbons; Landini; Lassus; Machaut; Marenzio; Morley; Obrecht; Ockeghem; Palestrina; La Rue; Tallis; Weelkes; Wilbye; Willaert.

Period: c.1600–c.1750
Movement: Baroque
Composers: Albinoni; Bach (JS); Buxtehude; Cavalli; Corelli; Couperin; Dowland; Gabrieli (D); Handel; Lully; Monteverdi; Purcell; Scarlatti; Scheidt; Schütz; Sweelinck; Telemann; Torelli; Vivaldi.

Period: c.1750–c.1830
Movement: Classical
Composers: Arne; Bach (CPE); Bach (JC); Beethoven; Bellini; Boccherini; Donizetti; Glinka; Gluck; Haydn; Hummel; Mozart; Paganini; Rossini; Schubert; Weber.

Period: early 19th century–early 20th century
Movement: Romantic
Composers: Berlioz; Berwald; Bizet; Borodin; Brahms; Bruckner; Busoni; Chopin; Debussy; Delibes; Dvořák; Elgar; Franck; Fauré; Gounod; Grieg; Liszt; Mahler; Massenet; Mendelssohn; Mussorgsky;

Offenbach; Puccini; Rachmaninov; Rimsky-Korsakov; Saint-Saëns; Satie; Schumann; Scriabin; Sibelius; Smetana; Strauss (J) II; Strauss (R); Tchaikovsky; Verdi; Wagner.

Period: c.1900–present
Movement: No specific title
Composers: Bartók; Bax; Berg; Berkeley; Britten; Cage; Copland; Delius; Gershwin; Glass; Hindemith; Holst; Honegger; Ives; Janáček; Kodály; Messaien; Milhaud; Nielsen; Nilsson; Poulenc; Prokofiev; Ravel; Reich; Schoenberg; Sessions; Shostakovich; Stockhausen; Stravinsky; Thomson; Tippett; Varèse; Vaughan Williams; Villa-Lobos; Walton; Webern; Weill.

POETS LAUREATE

In the 15thC Oxford and Cambridge universities gave the title 'laureate' to various poets. In 1668 the title gained its modern status when the poet John Dryden was granted a stipend and charged with writing court poetry and celebrating state occasions in verse.

Name	Appointed
Samuel Daniel	1599
Ben Jonson	1616
Sir William d'Avenant	1638
John Dryden	1668
Thomas Shadwell	1689
Nathan Tate	1692
Nicholas Rowe	1715
Rev. Laurence Eusden	1718
Colley Cibber	1730
William Whitehead	1757
Thomas Warton	1785
Henry James Pye	1790
Robert Southey	1813

Name	Appointed
William Wordsworth	1843
Alfred Lord Tennyson	1850
Alfred Austin	1896
Robert Bridges	1913
John Masefield	1930
Cecil Day Lewis	1968
Sir John Betjeman	1972
Edward (Ted) Hughes	1984

BOOKER PRIZE

Established in 1969 by Booker McConnell engineering company for British, Irish and Commonwealth fiction.

Year	Title	Author
1969	*Something to Answer*	P H Newby
1970	*The Elected Member*	Bernice Rubens
1971	*In a Free State*	V S Naipaul
1972	*G*	John Berger
1973	*The Siege of Krishnapur*	J G Farrell
1974	*The Conservationist*	Nadine Gordimer
	Holiday	Stanley Middleton
1975	*Heat and Dust*	Ruth Prawer Jhabvala
1976	*Saville*	David Storey
1977	*Staying On*	Paul Scott
1978	*The Sea, The Sea*	Iris Murdoch
1979	*Offshore*	Penelope Fitzgerald
1980	*Rites of Passage*	William Golding
1981	*Midnight's Children*	Salman Rushdie
1982	*Schindler's Ark*	Thomas Keneally
1983	*Life and Times of Michael K*	J M Coetzee
1984	*Hotel du Lac*	Anita Brookner
1985	*The Bone People*	Keri Hulme
1986	*The Old Devils*	Kingsley Amis

Year	Title	Author
1987	*Moon Tiger*	Penelope Lively
1988	*Oscar and Lucinda*	Peter Carey
1989	*The Remains of the Day*	Kazuo Ishiguro
1990	*Possession*	A S Byatt
1991	*The Famished Road*	Ben Okri
1992	*Sacred Hunger*	Barry Unsworth
	The English Patient	Michael Ondaatje
1993	*Paddy Clarke Ha Ha Ha*	Roddy Doyle
1994	*How Late It Was, How Late*	James Kelman
1995	*The Ghost Road*	Pat Barker

PULITZER PRIZE

Established in 1917 by Joseph Pulitzer for excellence in American literature.

Year	Title	Author
1981	*A Confederacy of Dunces*	John Kennedy Toole
1982	*Rabbit is Rich*	John Updike
1983	*The Color Purple*	Alice Walker
1984	*Ironweed*	William Kennedy
1985	*Foreign Affairs*	Alison Lurie
1986	*Lonesome Dove*	Larry McMurtry
1987	*A Summer to Memphis*	Peter Taylor
1988	*Beloved*	Toni Morrison
1989	*Breathing Lessons*	Anne Tyler
1990	*The Mambo Kings Play Songs of Love*	Oscar Hijelos
1991	*Rabbit at Rest*	John Updike
1992	*A Thousand Acres*	Jane Smiley
1993	*A Good Scent from a Strange Mountain*	Robert Olen Butler
1994	*The Shipping News*	E Annie Proulx
1995	*The Stone Diaries*	Carol Shields

PRIX GONCOURT

Annual Académie Goncourt prize for a French fiction work.

Year	Title	Author
1981	*Anne-Marie*	Lucien Bodard
1982	*Dans la main de l'ange*	Dominique Fernandez
1983	*Les égarés*	Frederick Tristan
1984	*L'amant*	Marguerite Duras
1985	*Les noces barbares*	Yann Queffelec
1986	*Valet de nuit*	Michel Host
1987	*La nuit sacrée*	Tahir Ben Jelloun
1988	*L'Exposition coloniale*	Erik Orsenna
1989	*Un grand pas vers le Bon Dieu*	Jean Vautrin
1990	*Les champs d'honneur*	Jean Rouault
1991	*Les filles du Calvaire*	Pierre Cambescot
1992	*Texaco*	Patrick Chamoiseau
1993	*Le Rocher de Tanios*	Amin Maalouf
1994	*Un aller simple*	Didier van Cauwelaert
1995	*Le testament français*	Andrei Makine

NOBEL PRIZE FOR LITERATURE

Year	Author	Year	Author
1901	Rene Sully Prudhomme	1914	*No award*
1902	Theodor Mommsen	1915	Romain Rolland
1903	Bjornestjerne Bjornson	1916	Verner Von Heidenstam
1904	Frederic Mistral/	1917	Karl Gjellerup/
	Juan Echegaray		Henrik Pontoppidan
1905	Henryk Sienkiewicz	1918	*No award*
1906	Giosue Carducci	1919	Carl Spitteler
1907	Rudyard Kipling	1920	Knut Hamsun
1908	Rudolf Eucken	1921	Anatole France
1909	Selma Lagerlof	1922	Jacinto Benavente
1910	Paul Von Heyse	1923	William Butler Yeats
1911	Maurice Maeterlinck	1924	Wladyslaw Reymont
1912	Gerhart Hauptmann	1925	George Bernard Shaw
1913	Sir Rabindranath Tagore	1926	Grazia Deledda

1927	Henri Bergson
1928	Sigrid Undset
1929	Thomas Mann
1930	Sinclair Lewis
1931	Erik Karlfeldt
1932	John Galsworthy
1933	Ivan Bunin
1934	Luigi Pirandello
1935	*No award*
1936	Eugene O'Neill
1937	Roger Martin du Gard
1938	Pearl S Buck
1939	Frans Eemil Sillanpää
1940–	
1943	*No award*
1944	Johannes V Jensen
1945	Gabriela Mistral
1946	Hermann Hesse
1947	André Gide
1948	Thomas Stearns Eliot
1949	William Faulkner
1950	Bertrand Russell
1951	Par Lagerkvist
1952	François Mauriac
1953	Sir Winston Churchill
1954	Ernest Hemingway
1955	Halidor Laxness
1956	Juan Ramón Jiménez
1957	Albert Camus
1958	Boris Pasternak (declined)
1959	Salvatore Quasimodo
1960	Saint-John Perse
1961	Ivo Andric
1962	John Steinbeck
1963	George Seferis
1964	Jean-Paul Sartre (declined)
1965	Mikhail Sholokhov
1966	Shmuel Yosef Agnonnelly Sachs
1967	Miguel Angel Asturias
1968	Yasunan Kawabata
1969	Samuel Beckett
1970	Alexander Solzhenitryn
1971	Pablo Neruda
1972	Heinrich Böll
1973	Patrick White
1974	Eyvind Johnson/Harry Edmund Martinson
1975	Eugenio Montale
1976	Saul Bellow
1977	V Alexandre
1978	Isaac Bashevis Singer
1979	Odysseus Alepoudhelis
1980	Czeslaw Milosz
1981	Elias Canetti
1982	Gabriel Garcia Márquez
1983	William Gerald Golding
1984	Jaraslav Seifert
1985	Claude Simon
1986	Wole Soyinka
1987	Joseph Brodsky
1988	Naguib Mahfouz
1989	Camilo José Cela
1990	Octavio Paz
1991	Nadine Gordimer
1992	Derek Walcott
1993	Toni Morrison
1994	Kenzaburo Oe
1995	Seamus Heaney

THE OSCARS

Year	Best film	Best actor
1927/8	*Wings*	Emil Jannings
1928/9	*Broadway Melody*	Warner Baxter
1929/30	*All Quiet on the Western Front*	George Arliss
1930/1	*Cimarron*	Lionel Barrymore
1931/2	*Grand Hotel*	Frederick March
		Wallace Beery
1932/3	*Cavalcade*	Charles Laughton
1934	*It Happened One Night*	Clark Gable
1935	*Mutiny on the Bounty*	Victor McLaglen
1936	*The Great Ziegfeld*	Paul Muni
1937	*The Life of Emile Zola*	Spencer Tracy
1938	*You Can't Take It With You*	Spencer Tracy
1939	*Gone with the Wind*	Robert Donat
1940	*Rebecca*	James Stewart
1941	*How Green Was My Valley*	Gary Cooper
1942	*Mrs Miniver*	James Cagney
1943	*Casablanca*	Paul Lukas
1944	*Going My Way*	Bing Crosby
1945	*The Lost Weekend*	Ray Milland
1946	*The Best Years of Our Lives*	Fredric March
1947	*Gentleman's Agreement*	Ronald Colman

Best actress	Best director
Janet Gaynor	Frank Borzage
Mary Pickford	Frank Lloyd
Norma Shearer	Lewis Milestone
Marie Dressler	Norman Taurog
Helen Hayes	Frank Borzage
Katharine Hepburn	Frank Lloyd
Claudette Colbert	Frank Capra
Bette Davis	John Ford
Luise Rainer	Frank Capra
Luise Rainer	Leo McCarey
Bette Davis	Frank Capra
Vivien Leigh	Victor Fleming
Ginger Rogers	John Ford
Joan Fontaine	John Ford
Greer Garson	William Wyler
Jennifer Jones	Michael Curtiz
Ingrid Bergman	Leo McCarey
Joan Crawford	Billy Wilder
Olivia de Havilland	William Wyler
Loretta Young	Elia Kazan

Year	Best film	Best actor
1948	*Hamlet*	Laurence Olivier
1949	*All the King's Men*	Broderick Crawford
1950	*All About Eve*	José Ferrer
1951	*An American in Paris*	Humphrey Bogart
1952	*The Greatest Show on Earth*	Gary Cooper
1953	*From Here to Eternity*	William Holden
1954	*On the Waterfront*	Marlon Brando
1955	*Marty*	Ernest Borgnine
1956	*Around the World in Eighty Days*	Yul Brynner
1957	*The Bridge on the River Kwai*	Alec Guinness
1958	*Gigi*	David Niven
1959	*Ben-Hur*	Charlton Heston
1960	*The Apartment*	Burt Lancaster
1961	*West Side Story*	Maximilian Schell
1962	*Lawrence of Arabia*	Gregory Peck
1963	*Tom Jones*	Sidney Poitier
1964	*My Fair Lady*	Rex Harrison
1965	*The Sound of Music*	Lee Marvin
1966	*A Man for All Seasons*	Paul Scofield
1967	*In the Heat of the Night*	Rod Steiger
1968	*Oliver*	Cliff Robertson
1969	*Midnight Cowboy*	John Wayne
1970	*Patton*	George C Scott

Best actress	Best director
Jane Wyman	John Huston
Olivia de Havilland	Joseph L Mankiewicz
Judy Holliday	Joseph L Mankiewicz
Vivien Leigh	George Stevens
Shirley Booth	John Ford
Audrey Hepburn	Fred Zinnemann
Grace Kelly	Elia Kazan
Anna Magnani	Delbert Mann
Ingrid Bergman	George Stevens
Joanne Woodward	David Lean
Susan Hayward	Vincente Minnelli
Simone Signoret	William Wyler
Elizabeth Taylor	Billy Wilder
Sophia Loren	Robert Wise
Anne Bancroft	David Lean
Patricia Neal	Tony Richardson
Julie Andrews	George Cukor
Julie Christie	Robert Wise
Elizabeth Taylor	Fred Zinnemann
Katharine Hepburn	Mike Nichols
Katharine Hepburn/	Carole Reed
Barbra Streisand	
Maggie Smith	John Schlesinger
Glenda Jackson	Franklin J Schaffner

Year	Best film	Best actor
1971	*The French Connection*	Gene Hackman
1972	*The Godfather*	Marlon Brando
1973	*The Sting*	Jack Lemmon
1974	*The Godfather Part II*	Art Carney
1975	*One Flew Over the Cuckoo's Nest*	Jack Nicholson
1976	*Rocky*	Peter Finch
1977	*Annie Hall*	Richard Dreyfuss
1978	*The Deer Hunter*	Jon Voight
1979	*Kramer vs Kramer*	Dustin Hoffman
1980	*Ordinary People*	Robert de Niro
1981	*Chariots of Fire*	Henry Fonda
1982	*Gandhi*	Ben Kingsley
1983	*Terms of Endearment*	Robert Duvall
1984	*Amadeus*	F Murray Abraham
1985	*Out of Africa*	William Hurt
1986	*Platoon*	Paul Newman
1987	*The Last Emperor*	Michael Douglas
1988	*Rain Man*	Dustin Hoffman
1989	*Driving Miss Daisy*	Daniel Day Lewis
1990	*Dances with Wolves*	Jeremy Irons
1991	*Silence of the Lambs*	Anthony Hopkins
1992	*Unforgiven*	Al Pacino
1993	*Schindler's List*	Tom Hanks
1994	*Forrest Gump*	Tom Hanks

Best actress	Best director
Jane Fonda	William Friedkin
Liza Minnelli	Bob Fosse
Glenda Jackson	George Roy Hill
Ellen Burstyn	Francis Ford Coppola
Louise Fletcher	Milos Forman
Faye Dunaway	John G Avildsen
Diane Keaton	Woody Allen
Jane Fonda	Michael Cimino
Sally Field	Robert Benton
Sissy Spacek	Robert Redford
Katharine Hepburn	Warren Beatty
Meryl Streep	Richard Attenborough
Shirley Maclaine	James L Brooks
Sally Field	Milos Forman
Geraldine Page	Sydney Pollack
Marlee Matlin	Oliver Stone
Cher	Bernardo Bertolucci
Jodie Foster	Barry Levinson
Jessica Tandy	Oliver Stone
Kathy Bates	Kevin Costner
Jodie Foster	Jonathan Demme
Emma Thompson	Clint Eastwood
Holly Hunter	Steven Spielberg
Jessica Lange	Robert Zemeckis

Language

TOP TEN LANGUAGES

Name	Speakers (millions)
Mandarin	600
English	400
Spanish	300
Hindi	290
Arabic	230
Russian	160
Portuguese	150
Bengali	145
German	120
Japanese	120

TYPOGRAPHIC, SCIENTIFIC AND MATHEMATICAL SYMBOLS

+	Addition	−	Subtraction
×	Multiplication	÷	Division
=	Equals	≠	Does not equal
≡	Identical; congruent	≈	Approximately equals
>	Greater than	<	Less than
≫	Much greater than	≪	Much less than
≯	Not greater than	≮	Not less than
≅	Isomorphic	:	Ratio
::	Used between ratios	∞	Infinity
∴	Therefore	∵	Since; because

$\Rightarrow$	Gives; leads on to	$\angle$	Angle
$\llcorner$	Right angle	$\perp$	Perpendicular
∇	Nablus	∂	Differential
δ	Delta	λ	Lambda
ε	Epsilon	ν	Nu
μ	Mu	$\lessgtr$	Greater or less than
$\parallel$	Parallel	$\bigcirc$	Circle
	Arc	$\triangle$	Triangle
$\square$	Square	$\square$	Rectangle
$\square$	Parallelogram	$\sqrt{}$	Square Root
Σ	Sum	$\int$	Integral
$\cup$	Union	$\cap$	Intersection
$\in$	Belongs to	$\subset$	A subset of
$\{\}$	Set braces	$\varnothing$	Empty set absolute value
$\triangleleft$	Normal subgroup of	μ	Mean (population)
σ	Standard deviation (population)	$\bar{x}$	Mean (sample)
s	Standard deviation (sample)	π	Ratio of circumference of any circle to its diameter
e	Base of natural logarithms	iff	If and only if
$\forall$	For all	λ	Wavelength

Å	Angstrom unit	μ	Magnetic permeability
Ω	Ohm	h	Planck constant
p	Radius of curvature	&	Ampersand
&c	Etcetera	<	Derived from
{}	Braces	()	Parentheses
[]	Square brackets		

ACCENTS

Name	Character	Example
Acute	´	é
Angstrom	°	å
Asper	ʻ	ʻo
Breve	˘	ă
Cedilla	¸	ç
Circumflex	^	î
Diaeresis	¨	ï
Haček	ˇ	č
Lenis	'	'o
Macron	‾	ā
Tilde	~	ñ
Umlaut	¨	ü

THE APOSTROPHE

One of the most ill-used punctuation marks in the
English language.
It is used:

1. To show the possessive case

a   The apostrophe for this should only be used for proper and
common nouns and not for the following pronouns: hers, its
(it's = it is), ours, theirs, yours.

b   In nouns (sing. and plural) that end in a letter other than *s*, the
apostrophe must precede the added *s*, as in the chief's tent, men's
boots, the fox's earth.

c   In nouns (sing.) that end in *s*, the possessive is usually formed
by adding the *'s*, as in the octopus's tentacles.

d   In nouns (plural) that end in *s*, the apostrophe must follow the
s, as in the boys' clothing, the octopuses' tentacles.

e   When the added *s* is silent in speech it is usually omitted, as in
for goodness' sake.

f   In English names and surnames add *'s*, as in Burns's poems,
St James's Road; but sound often demands the omission of
another *s*, as in Bridges' poems.

g   Ancient names ending in *s* usually omit a further *s*, as in Moses'
law, Jesus' love.

h   Abbreviations add *'s* when singular, as in the MP's constituency,
and *s'*, when plural, as in MPs' salaries.

2. To show omission

Examples: e'er (ever), tho' (though), he's (he is, he has), it's (it is),
'67 (1967 or contextual century).

Apostrophes in abbreviations similar to the following
should join close up to the letters

don't (do not)	haven't (have not)	shan't (shall not)
shouldn't (should not)	won't (will not)	isn't (is not)
doesn't (does not)	daren't (dare not)	couldn't (could not)
can't (cannot)	mustn't (must not)	hasn't (has not)
there'll (there will)	I'll (I will)	we'll (we will)
you'll (you will)	who'll (who will)	they'll (they will)
I'd (I had, would)	who'd (who would)	I'm (I am)
you're (you are)	who's (who is, *not* pronoun, i.e. whose is that?)	

But note:
couldst   canst   shouldst   wouldst

3. Irish names
Example: O'Reilly.

CHINESE: WADE-GILES v PINYIN
The Romanization of Chinese
For English speakers the most common romanization
system is the Wade-Giles system. The New China News
Agency has issued insights into the system used
internally in the People's Republic. It is called Pinyin and
it is intended that some day Chinese characters can be
abolished in favour of this method. (However, this will be
difficult as long as various dialects are still in use.)
Following are listed some names of people and places
under the two romanization methods.

Old: Wade-Giles	**New: Pinyin**
Names	
Chiang Ch'ing	Jiang Qing
Chou En-lai	Zhou Enlai
Hua Kuo-feng	Hua Guofeng
Mao Tse-Tung	Mao Zedong
Teng Hsiao-P'ing	Deng Xiaoping
Provinces	
Anwei	Anhui
Chekiang	Zhejiang
Fukien	Fujian
Heilungkiang	Heilongjiang
Honan	Henan
Hopei	Hebei
Hunan	Hunan
Hupei	Hubei
Kansu	Gansu
Kiangsi	Jiangxi
Kiangsu	Jiangsu
Kirin	Jilin
Kwangsi	Guangxi
Kwangtung	Guangdong
Kweichow	Guizhou
Liaoning	Liaoning
Ningsia	Ningxia
Shansi	Shanxi
Shantung	Shandong
Shensi	Shaanxi
Sinkiang	Xinjiang
Szechwan	Sichuan
Tsinghai	Qinghai
Yunnan	Yunnan

Cities

Canton	Guangzhou
Chengtu	Chengdu
Chungking	Chongqing
Hangchow	Hangzhou
Nanking	Nanjing
Peking	Beijing
Shanghai	Shanghai
Sian	Xi'an
Sochow	Suzhou
Tientsin	Tianjin
Tsingtao	Qingdao
Wuhan	Wuhan

Rivers

Hwang Ho	Huang Ho
Yangtze	Yangzi or Chang

AMERICAN SPELLING AND WORD VARIATIONS

British	American	British	American
aeroplane	airplane	colour	color
aluminium	aluminum	cosy	cozy
armoury	armory	courgette	zucchini
biscuit	cookie	defence	defense
calibre	caliber	demagogue	demagog
callipers	calipers	dialling	dialing
callisthenics	calisthenics	dialogue	dialog
car bonnet	hood	draughts (game)	checkers
car boot	car trunk	endeavour	endeavor
car bumper	fender	enfold	infold
catalogue	catalog	enrolled	enroled
centre	center	epilogue	epilog
cheque	check	faeces	feces

British	American	British	American
favour	favor	paediatrics	pediatrics
fervour	fervor	paraffin	kerosene
flavour	flavor	pavement	sidewalk
foetus	fetus	pedlar	peddler
gelatine	gelatin	petrol	gas(oline)
glycerine	glycerin	plough	plow
grey	gray	pretence	pretense
gynaecology	gynecology	programme	program
haemorrhage	hemorrhage	pyjamas	pajamas
harbour	harbor	rateable	ratable
honour	honor	reconnoitre	reconnoiter
humour	humor	rigour	rigor
kerb	curb	saleable	salable
ketchup	catchup	sanatorium	sanitarium
licence	license	sceptic	skeptic
liquorice	licorice	sulphur	sulfur
manoeuvre	maneuver	sweets	candies
meagre	meager	tap	faucet
metre	meter	theatre	theater
mould	mold	traveller	traveler
nappy	diaper	trousers	pants
neighbour	neighbor	tumour	tumor
ochre	ocher	valour	valor
offence	offense	waistcoat	vest
organdie	organdy	wallet	billfold
orthopaedic	orthopedic	whisky	whiskey

ABBREVIATIONS (DEGREES, QUALIFICATIONS, MEMBERSHIPS, ASSOCIATIONS)

Note: The following list contains only the most common abbreviations; several organizations offer different categories of membership (e.g. associate membership, fellowship) but to avoid repetition only one membership category is shown here.

ACTT	Association of Cinematograph, Television and Allied Technicians
ADI	Approved Driving Instructor
ADO	Association of Dispensing Opticians
ATD	Art Teacher's Diploma
ATPL	Airline Transport Pilot's Licence
BA	Bachelor of Arts
BAc	Bachelor of Acupuncture
BAcc	Bachelor of Accountancy
BAC	British Accreditation Council of Independent Further and Higher Education
BA(Lan)	Bachelor of Languages
BALPA	British Airline Pilots' Association
BArch	Bachelor of Architecture
BCL	Bachelor of Civil Law
BCS	Bachelor of Combined Studies/Chemical Science
BD	Bachelor of Divinity
BDS	Bachelor of Dental Surgery
BEd	Bachelor of Education
BEng	Bachelor of Engineering
BEng and Man	Bachelor of Mechanical Engineering, Manufacture and Management
BER	Board of Engineers' Registration
BHSI	British Horse Society's Instructor's Certificate
BLib	Bachelor of Library Science
BLitt	Bachelor of Letters/Literature
BMed	Bachelor of Medicine
BMedSci	Bachelor of Medical Science
BMus	Bachelor of Music
BPharm	Bachelor of Pharmacy
BPhil	Bachelor of Philosophy
BSc	Bachelor of Science
BSc(Eng)	Bachelor of Science in Engineering
BTEC	Business and Technician Education Council

BTech	Bachelor of Technology
BTh	Bachelor of Theology
CA	Member of the Institute of Chartered Accountants of Scotland
CACC	Council for the Accreditation of Correspondence Colleges
CBiol	Chartered Biologist
CCETSW	Central Council for Education and Training in Social Work
CChem	Chartered Chemist
CCol	Chartered Colourist
CEng	Chartered Engineer
CertEd	Certificate in Education
CETHV	Certificate of Education in Training as a Health Visitor
C&G	City and Guilds of London Institute
ChB	Bachelor of Surgery
ChM	Master of Surgery
CHP	Certificate in Hypnosis and Psychology
CIFE	Conference for Independent Further Education
CMA	Certificate in Management Accountancy
CMS	Certificate in Management Studies
CNAA	Council for National Academic Awards
CPA	Chartered Patent Agent
CPL	Commercial Pilot's Licence
CSE	Certificate of Secondary Education
CSS	Certificate in Social Service
CSYS	Certificate in Sixth Year Studies
CTEFLA	Certificate in Teaching English as a Foreign Language Abroad
DA	Diploma in Anaesthetics/Art
DAvMed	Diploma in Aviation Medicine
DBO	Diploma of the British Orthoptic Society
DCG	Diploma in Careers Guidance

DCH	Diploma in Child Health
DCL	Doctor of Civil Laws
DCLP	Diploma in Contact Lens Practice
DCR(R) or (T)	Diploma of the College of Radiographers
DD	Doctor of Divinity
DDPH	Diploma in Dental Public Health
DDS	Doctor of Dental Surgery
DDSc	Doctor of Dental Science
DES	Department of Education and Science
DHP	Diploma in Hypnosis and Psychotherapy
DIA	Diploma of Industrial Administration/Driving Instructors' Association
DIH	Diploma in Industrial Health
DipAD	Diploma in Art and Design
DipAE	Diploma in Adult Education
DipAT	Diploma in Accounting Technology
DipBact	Diploma in Bacteriology
DipCAM	Diploma of the Communication, Advertising and Marketing Education Foundation
DipCD	Diploma in Community Development
DipClinPath	Diploma in Clinical Pathology
DipCom	Diploma in/of Commerce
DipCOT	Diploma of the College of Occupational Therapists
DipCT	Diploma in Corporate Treasury Management
DipEd	Diploma in Education
DipEF	Diploma in Executive Finance
DipEH	Diploma in Environmental Health
DipEMA	Diploma in Executive and Management Accountancy
DipEng	Diploma in Engineering
DipEngLit	Diploma in English Literature
DipFD	Diploma in Funeral Directing, National Association of Funeral Directors
DipFS	Diploma in Financial Studies
DipHE	Diploma of Higher Education

DipM	Diploma in Marketing, Institute of Marketing
DipPharmMed	Diploma in Pharmaceutical Medicine
DipRADA	Diploma of the Royal Academy of Dramatic Art
DipRAM	Diploma of the Royal Academy of Music
DipRSAMD	Diploma of the Royal Scottish Academy of Music and Drama
DipTESOL	Diploma in Teaching English to Speakers of Other Languages
DipTHP	Diploma in Therapeutic Hypnosis and Psychotherapy
DipTM	Diploma in Training Management, the Institute of Training and Development
DipUniv	Diploma of the University
DipYD	Diploma of Youth Development
DLit(t)	Doctor of Letters or Literature
DLO	Doctor of Laryngology and Otology
DMRT	Diploma in Radiotherapy
DMS	Diploma in Management Studies
DMus	Doctor of Music
DO	Diploma in Ophthalmology/Osteopathy
DOpt	Diploma in Ophthalmic Optics
DOrth	Diploma in Orthoptics/Orthodontics
DP	Diploma in Psychotherapy
DPA	Diploma in Public Administration
DPH	Diploma in Public Health
DPhil	Doctor of Philosophy
DrAc	Doctor of Acupuncture
DRCOG	Diploma of the Royal College of Obstetricians and Gynaecologists
DRE	Diploma in Remedial Electrolysis, Institute of Electrolysis
DSc	Doctor of Science
DSc(Econ)	Doctor of Science (Economics) or in Economics
DTech	Doctor of Technology
DTI	Department of Trade and Industry

DTp	Department of Transport
	Doctor of the University
DVetMed, DVM, DVM&S, DVS, DVSc	Doctor of Veterinary Medicine, Medicine and Surgery, Surgery, Surgery and Veterinary Science
EC	Engineering Council
EN	Enrolled Nurse
ENB	English National Board of Nursing, Midwifery and Health Visiting
EN(G)	Enrolled Nurse (General)
EngTech	Engineering Technician
EN(M)	Enrolled Nurse (Mental)
EN(MH)	Enrolled Nurse (Mental handicap)
FBA	Fellow of the British Academy
FBHS	Fellow of the British Horse Society
FCAM	Fellow of the Communication, Advertising and Marketing Education Foundation
FCI	Fellow of the Institute of Commerce
FCIM	Fellow of the Chartered Institute of Marketing
FCIT	Fellow of the Chartered Institute of Transport
FEIS	Fellow of the Educational Institute of Scotland
FGA	Fellow of the Gemmological Association
FIA	Fellow of the Institute of Actuaries
FICM	Fellow of the Institute of Credit Management
FRAS	Fellow of the Royal Astronomical Society
FRCA	Fellow of the Royal College of Art
FRCGP	Fellow of the Royal College of General Practitioners
FRCM	Fellow of the Royal College of Music
FRCR	Fellow of the Royal College of Radiologists
FRHistS	Fellow of the Royal Historical Society
FRHS	Fellow of the Royal Horticultural Society
FRIBA	Fellow of the Royal Institute of British Architects
FRICS	Fellow of the Royal Institution of Chartered Surveyors
FRPS	Fellow of the Royal Photographic Society

FRS	Fellow of the Royal Society
FRSCM	Fellow of the Royal School of Church Music
FSCA	Fellow of the Institute of Company Accountants
FSS	Fellow of the Royal Statistical Society
HNC	Higher National Certificate
HND	Higher National Diploma
HSC	Health and Safety Commission
ICSA	Institute of Chartered Secretaries and Administrators
IEng	Incorporated Engineer
IPFA	Member of Chartered Institute of Public Finance and Accountancy
JP	Justice of the Peace
LittB	Bachelor of Letters/Literature
LittD	Doctor of Letters/Literature
LLB	Bachelor of Laws
LLD	Doctor of Laws
LLM	Master of Laws
MA	Master of Arts
MABE	Member of the Association of Business Executives
MACP	Member of the Association of Computer Professionals
MAgr, MAgrSC	Master of Agriculture, Agricultural Science
MAIE	Member of the British Association of Industrial Editors
MAppSc	Master of Applied Science
MAPSAS	Member of the Association of Public Service Administrative Staff
MArb	Master of Arboriculture
MArch	Master of Architecture
MArt RCA	Master of Arts, Royal College of Art
MASI	Member of the Architects' and Surveyors' Institute
MBA	Master of Business Administration
MBAE	Member of the British Academy of Experts; Member of the British Association of Electrolysis

MB, BCh, MB, BChir, MB, BS, MB, ChB	Conjoint Degree of Bachelor of Medicine, Bachelor of Surgery
MBCO	Member of the British College of Ophthalmic Opticians
MBCS	Member of the British Computer Society
MBEI	Member of the British Institute of Body Engineers
MBHA	Member of the British Hypnotherapy Association
MBHI	Member of the British Horological Institute
MBID	Member of the British Institute of Interior Design
MBIE	Member of the British Institute of Embalmers
MBII	Member of the British Institute of Innkeeping
MBIM	Member of the British Institute of Management
MBT	Member of the Association of Beauty Teachers
MCFI	Member of the Clothing and Footwear Institute
MCh, MChir, MChur	Master of Surgery
MChD	Master of Dental Surgery
MChS	Member of the Society of Chiropodists
MCIBS	Member of the Chartered Institute of Bankers in Scotland
MCIBSE	Member of the Chartered Institution of Building Services Engineers
MCIM	Member of the Chartered Institute of Marketing
MCIOB	Member of the Chartered Institute of Building
MCIT	Member of the Chartered Institute of Transport
MComm	Master of Commerce
MD	Doctor of Medicine
MDS	Master of Dental Surgery
MEd	Master of Education
MEng	Master of Engineering
MFCM	Member of the Faculty of Community Medicine
MFDO	Member of the Faculty of Dispensing Opticians
MFHom	Member of the Faculty of Homeopathy

MHCIMA	Member of the Hotel, Catering and Institutional Management Association
MHFS	Member of the Council of Health Fitness and Sports Therapists
MIAA (Architects)	Member of the Incorporated Association of Architects and Surveyors
MIAB	Member of the International Association of Book-keepers
MIAgrE	Member of the Institution of Agricultural Engineers
MIAP	Member of the Institution of Analysts and Programmers
MIAS (Surveyors)	Member of the Incorporated Association of Architects and Surveyors
MIAT	Member of the Institute of Animal Technology
MIBC	Member of the Institute of Building Control
MIBCO	Member of the Institution of Building Control Officers
MIBiol	Member of the Institute of Biology
MICE	Member of the Institution of Civil Engineers
MIChemE	Member of the Institution of Chemical Engineers
MICO	Member of the Institute of Careers Officers
MIDPM	Member of the International Dance Teachers' Association
MIED	Member of the Institution of Engineering Designers
MIEE	Member of the Institution of Electrical Engineers
MIEx	Member of the Institute of Export
MIFireE	Member of the Institution of Fire Engineers
MIGasE	Member of the Institution of Gas Engineers
MIGeol	Member of the Institute of Geologists
MIH	Member of the Institute of Housing
MIHEc	Member of the Institute of Home Economics
MIIA	Member of the Institute of Internal Auditors
MIInfSc	Member of the Institute of Information Scientists
MIIRSM	Member of the International Institute of Risk and Safety Management

MIISE	Member of the International Institute of Social Economics
MIL	Member of the Institute of Linguists
MILAM	Member of the Institute of Leisure and Amenity Management
MIM	Member of the Institute of Metals
MIManf	Member of the Institute of Manufacturing
MIMarE	Member of the Institute of Marine Engineers
MIMatM	Member of the Institute of Materials Management
MIMBM	Member of the Institute of Maintenance and Building Management
MIMC	Member of the Institute of Management Consultants
MIMechE	Member of the Institution of Mechanical Engineers
MIMechIE	Member of the Institution of Mechanical Incorporated Engineers
MIMI	Member of the Institute of the Motor Industry
MIMinE	Member of the Institution of Mining Engineers
MIMIT	Member of the Institute of Musical Instrument Technology
MIMM	Member of the Institute of Massage and Movement; Member of the Institution of Mining and Metallurgy
MIMS	Member of the Institute of Management Specialists
MInstAM	Member of the Institute of Administrative Management
MInstBB	Member of the Institute of British Bakers
MInstBCA	Member of the Institute of Burial and Cremation Administration
MInstBE	Member of the Institute of British Engineers
MInstBRM	Member of the Institute of Baths and Recreation Management
MInstCh	Member of the Institute of Chiropodists
MInstD	Member of the Institute of Directors
MInstE	Member of the Institute of Energy
MIFF	Member of the Institute of Freight Forwarders
MInstGasE	Member of the Institute of Gas Engineers

MInstMC	Member of the Institute of Measurement and Control
MInstNDT	Member of the Institute of Non-Destructive Testing
MInstP	Member of the Institute of Physics
MInstPet	Member of the Institute of Petroleum
MInstPkg	Member of the Institute of Packaging
MInstR	Member of the Institute of Refrigeration
MInstSMM	Member of the Institute of Sales and Marketing Management
MInstTA	Member of the Institute of Transport Administration
MInstWM	Member of the Institute of Waste Management
MIOB	Member of the Institute of Building
MIOC	Member of the Institute of Carpenters
MIOFMS	Member of the Institute of Financial and Management Studies
MIOP	Member of the Institute of Printing
MIOSH	Member of the Institution of Occupational Safety and Health
MIP	Member of the Institute of Plumbing
MIPA	Member of the Institute of Practitioners in Advertising
MIPC	Member of the Institute of Production Control
MIPHE	Member of the Institute of Public Health Engineers
MIPI	Member of the Institute of Professional Investigators
MIPlantE	Member of the Institution of Plant Engineers
MIPM	Member of the Institute of Personnel Management
MIPR	Member of the Institute of Public Relations
MIProdE	Member of the Institution of Production Engineers
MIQ	Member of the Institute of Quarrying
MIQA	Member of the Institute of Quality Assurance
MIR	Member of the Institute of Population Registration
MIRRV	Member of the Institute of Revenue, Rating and Valuation
MIRSE	Member of the Institution of Railway Signal Engineers
MIRSO	Member of the Institute of Road Safety Officers

MIS	Member of the Institute of Statisticians
MISM	Member of the Institute of Supervisory Management
MISOB	Member of the Incorporated Society of Organ Builders
MIStructE	Member of the Institution of Structural Engineers
MISW	Member of the Institute of Social Welfare
MITD	Member of the Institute of Training and Development
MITSA	Member of the Institute of Trading Standards Administration
MIWEM	Member of the Institution of Water and Environmental Management
MIWPC	Member of the Institute of Water Pollution Control
MLA	Master in Landscape Architecture
MLCOM	Member of the London College of Osteopathic Medicine
MLib	Master of Librarianship
MLing	Master of Languages
MLitt	Master of Letters/Literature
MMS	Member of the Institute of Management Services
MMus	Master of Music
MNAEA	Member of the National Association of Estate Agents
MNI	Member of the Nautical Institute
MNIMH	Member of the National Institute of Medical Herbalists
MPharm	Master of Pharmacy
MPhil	Master of Philosophy
MPRI	Member of the Plastics and Rubber Institute
MRAeS	Member of the Royal Aeronautical Society
MRCGP	Member of the Royal College of General Practitioners
MRCOG	Member of the Royal College of Obstetricians and Gynaecologists

MRCP	Member of the Royal College of Physicians of London
MRCPath	Member of the Royal College of Pathologists
MRCPsych	Member of the Royal College of Psychiatrists
MRCP(UK)	Member of the Royal College of Physicians of the United Kingdom
MRCSEng	Member of the Royal College of Surgeons of England
MRCVS	Member of the Royal College of Veterinary Surgeons
MRIN	Member of the Royal Institute of Navigation
MRINA	Member of the Royal Institution of Naval Architects
MRIPHH	Member of the Royal Institute of Public Health and Hygiene
MRO	Member of the Register of Osteopaths
MRPharms	Member of the Royal Pharmaceutical Society
MRSC	Member of the Royal Society of Chemistry
MRSH	Member of the Royal Society of Health
MRTPI	Member of the Royal Town Planning Institute
MSBP	Member of the Society of Business Practitioners
MSBT	Member of the Society of Business Teachers
MSc	Master of Science
MSc(Econ)	Master of Science in Economics
MSCT	Member of the Society of Cardiological Technicians
MSE	Member of the Society of Engineers
MSIAD	Member of the Society of Industrial Artists and Designers
MSocSt	Master of Social Studies
MSSCh	Member of the School of Surgical Chiropody
MSSF	Member of the Society of Shoe Fitters
MSST	Member of the Society of Surveying Technicians
MSTA	Member of the Swimming Teachers' Association
MTech	Master of Technology
MTh	Master of Theology
MUniv	Master of the University (Honorary)

MusB	Bachelor of Music
MusD	Doctor of Music
MusM	Master of Music
MVM	Master of Veterinary Medicine
MVS(c)	Master of Veterinary Science
MWeldI	Member of the Welding Institute
MWES	Member of the Women's Engineering Society
MYD	Member of the Youth Development Association
NCC	National Computing Centre
NCVQ	National Council for Vocational Qualifications
NNEB	National Nursery Examination Board
NVQ	National Vocational Qualification
PGCE	Postgraduate Certificate in Education
PhD	Doctor of Philosophy
PPL	Private Pilot's Licence
QC	Queen's Counsel
RA	Royal Academician
RANA	Royal Animal Nursing Auxiliary
RFInstCF	Registered Fitter of the National Institute of Carpet Fitters
RGN	Registered General Nurse
RHV	Registered Health Visitor
RM	Registered Midwife
RMN	Registered Mental Nurse
RNMH	Registered Nurse for the Mentally Handicapped
RP	Registered Plumber
RSA	Royal Society of Arts
RSCN	Registered Sick Children's Nurse
ScD	Doctor of Science
SCOTVEC	Scottish Vocational Education Council
SCPL	Senior Commercial Pilot's Licence
SLC	Secretarial Language Certificate
SLD	Secretarial Language Diploma
SNC	Scottish National Certificate
SND	Scottish National Diploma

SNNEB	Scottish Nursery Nurses' Examination Board
SRCh	State Registered Chiropodist
SRCN	State Registered Children's Nurse
SRD	State Registered Dietitian
TCert	Teacher's Certificate
TD	Technician Diploma
TEFL	Teaching English as a Foreign Language
UCAS	The Universities and Colleges Admissions Services
UGC	University Grants Committee
UKCC	United Kingdom Central Council for Nursing, Midwifery and Health Visiting

BRANCHES OF STUDY

Name	Field of Study
Abiology	Inanimate objects
Acarology	Mites, ticks
Actinology	Chemical effects of light in certain wavelengths
Adenology	Glands
Aeroballistics	Science of ballistics as applied to aerodynamics
Aerodynamics	Motions of air and gases, especially in relation to moving objects
Aerography	Atmospheric conditions
Aerolithology	Meteors
Aerolitics	Aerolites (stormy meteors)
Aerology	Planet Mars
Aerometry	Properties of air
Aeronautics	Technology of flying aeroplanes
Aerophysics	Earth's atmosphere (especially effects of high-speed flying bodies)
Aerostatics	Construction/operation of lighter-than-air craft such as balloons
Aesthetics	Principles of beauty and the beautiful
Aetiology	Philosophy of causation

Name	Field of Study
Agmatology	Bone fractures
Agriology	Comparative study of the customs of primitive peoples
Agrobiology	Soil management
Agrogeology	Adaptability of land to agriculture
Agrology	Crop production
Agronomy	Management in farming
Agrostology	Grasses (*also called* graminology)
Alethiology	Branch of logic concerned with truth and error
Algebra	Branch of mathematics which uses letters and other symbols to represent numbers, values, etc.
Algology	Seaweeds and algae
Alimentology	Nutrition (*also called* trophology)
Allergology	Allergies
Ambrology	Sources/formation of amber
Ampelography	Grapes
Amphibiology	Amphibians
Anatomy	Human body and its parts
Anemology	Winds
Angiology	Blood vessels and lymphatic system
Anthoecology	Flowers and their environment
Anthropometry	Proportions, size and weight of human body
Anthropogeny	Human origins
Anthropogeography	Geographical distribution of mankind and its relationship with the environment
Anthropography	Geographical distribution of different races
Anthropology	Mankind, especially origins and customs
Anthroposociology	Sociology of race using anthropological methods
Antinology	Chemical effects of light in certain wavelengths
Apiology	Honey bees
Apologetics	Defences or proofs of Christianity
Arachnology	Spiders

Name	Field of Study
Archaeogeology	Geological features of distant past
Archaeology	Human remains and artefacts
Architectonics	(1) Systematization of knowledge
	(2) Science of architecture
Archology	(1) Science of origins
	(2) Science of government
Areology	Planet Mars
Aretaics	Study of virtue
Arthrology	Joints of the body
Assyriology	Ancient Assyria
Astrogation	Space navigation
Astrogeology	Geological features of celestial bodies, especially the moon and solar planets
Astrognosy	Fixed stars
Astrolithology	Meteorites (*also called* meteoritics)
Astronautics	Space travel
Astronomy	Celestial bodies
Astrophysics	Origins and physical nature of celestial bodies
Atmology	Water vapour
Audiology	Hearing (especially impaired)
Autecology	Ecology of an individual plant or species
Autoecology	Relation of organisms to their environment
Avigation	Aerial navigation
Avionics	Electrical/electronic equipment used in aviation
Axiology	Values (ethics, aesthetics, religion, etc.)
Azoology	Inanimate nature
Bacteriology	Bacteria
Ballistics	Projectiles and firearms
Batology	Brambles
Bibliography	History of books
Bibliology	Doctrines of Bible
Bibliotics	Analysis of handwriting, especially manuscripts

Name	Field of Study
Bioastronautics	Effects of space travel, especially on human body
Biochemistry	Chemical processes in living organisms
Bioclimatology	Relationship between living creatures and atmospheric conditions
Biodynamics	Physiological processes of plants and animals
Bioecology	Interrelationship of plant and animal life in a shared environment
Biogeography	Geographical distribution of plants and animals
Biolinguistics	Relationship between physiology and speech
Biology	All living organisms
Bionics	How living creatures perform tasks and how this knowledge can be applied to automated or computer-driven equipment
Bionomics	*See* ecology
Biophysiology	Growth, structure and physiology of organs
Biostatics	Relationship between structure and function of plants and animals
Biotechnology	*See* ergonomics
Botany	All plant life (*also called* phytology)
Bryology	Mosses and liverworts
Cacogenics	Factors that influence degeneration in offspring, especially with respect to different races
Cambistry	Commercial exchange, especially international money values
Cardioangiology	Heart and blood vessels
Cardiodynamics	Forces and movements of the heart
Cardiology	Heart and its functions
Caricology	Sedges
Carpology	Fruits and seeds
Cartography	Map-making

Name	Field of Study
Casuistry	Relationship of general ethical principles to particular problems
Catoptrics	Light reflection
Cecidiology	Galls produced on trees by fungi, etc.
Cetology	Whales
Chemistry	Composition, properties and behaviour of substances
Chondrology	Cartilage
Chorology	Migrations and distributions of organisms
Chrematistics	Wealth
Christology	Nature and attitudes of Christ
Chromatology	Colours
Chrysology	Production of wealth, especially related to precious metals
Cinematography	Art of making cinema films
Climatology	Climates
Cliometrics	Application of mathematical principles to the study of history
Coccidology	Coccidea family (scales, mealy bugs, etc.)
Codicology	Early manuscripts
Coleopterology	Beetles, weevils
Conchology	Mollusc shells (*also called* malacology)
Cosmology	(1) Overall structure of physical universe (astronomy) (2) Origin, structure and evolution of universe (philosophy)
Criminology	Crime and criminals
Crustaceology	Crustaceans
Crustalogy	Surface of earth or moon
Cryogenics	Low temperatures and their effects
Cryology	Snow, ice
Cryptography	Secret writing, codes
Ctetology	Origin and development of acquired characteristics

Name	Field of Study
Cultural anthropology	Creative achievements of societies
Cybernetics	Comparative study of complex electronic machines and human nervous system
Cynology	Dogs
Cytochemistry	Chemistry of living cells
Cytology	Cells
Cytotechnology	Human cells, especially to detect cancer
Dactylography	Fingerprints
Dactylology	Sign language using hands
Demography	Vital and social statistics of populations
Demology	Human activities and social environments
Demonology	Demons
Dendrochronology	Examination of annual growth rings in trees to determine age
Dendrology	Trees
Deontology	Ethics
Dermatology	Skin, skin diseases
Desmidiology	Microscopic, unicellular algae
Desmopathology	Diseases of ligaments and tendons
Diabology	The Devil
Diagnostics	Diagnosis of illness/diseases
Didactics	Art/science of teaching
Dioptrics	Light refraction
Diplomatology	Analysis of original texts or documents
Dipterology	Diptera family (flies, mosquitoes, gnats, etc.)
Ecclesiology	Church building and decoration
Eccrinology	Secretions and secretory glands
Echinology	Sea urchins
Ecology	Relationship of living organisms to their environment (*also called* bionomics)
Economics	Production and distribution of wealth
Egyptology	Ancient Egypt

Name	Field of Study
Electrobiology	Electrical activity in organisms/effect of electricity on organisms
Emblematology	Interpretation of emblems
Emetology	Causes of vomiting
Emmenology	Menstruation
Endocrinology	Endocrine glands
Enterology	Intestines
Entomology	Insects (*also called* insectology)
Enzymology	Fermentation and enzymes (*also called* zymology)
Epidemiology	Incidence, distribution, control and prevention of diseases
Epigraphy	Deciphering and interpreting ancient inscriptions
Epiphytology	Plant diseases
Epistemology	Human knowledge, especially methods and validity of
Epizoology	Incidence and spread of animal diseases
Eremology	Deserts
Ergology	Physical and mental effects of work
Ergonomics	Relationship of man to his working environment (*also called* biotechnology)
Eschatology	Death and final destiny
Ethics	Moral principles and right action
Ethnology	Origin and development of all races and their relationships with each other
Ethology	Animal behaviour in relation to the environment
Etiology	Causes of diseases and why they spread
Etruscology	Etruscan civilization
Etymology	Origin and history of words
Eugenics	Improvement of a breed or species through selective breeding

Name	Field of Study
Euthenics	Improvement of a race or breed by controlling external influences such as environment
Exegetics	Interpretation of biblical literature
Exobiology	Life beyond earth's atmosphere
Faunology	*See* zoogeography
Filicology	Ferns (*also called* pteridology)
Fluviology	Watercourses, rivers
Foetology	Foetuses
Fromology	Cheese
Gastrology	Stomach functions and diseases
Gemmology	Gemstones
Genecology	Animal species and their environments
Genesiology	Human reproduction
Genetics	Heredity
Geodynamics	Forces within the earth
Geognosy	Constituent parts of the earth
Geogony	Formation of the earth
Geology	The earth
Geometry	Properties and relationships of angles, points, lines, surfaces and solids
Geomorphology	Earth's surface
Geratology	Ageing
Geriatrics	Care of the aged
Gerodontics	Dental problems of the aged
Glaciology	Glaciers
Glottogony	Origin of language
Glottology	Science of linguistics
Gnoseology	Philosophy of knowledge
Graminology	*See* agrostology
Grammar	Formal structure of a language
Graphology	Analysis of handwriting

Name	Field of Study
Gynaecology	Disorders of the female reproductive system
Gyniatrics	Women's diseases
Gyrostatics	Rotating solid bodies
Haematology	Blood, diseases of the blood and blood-forming tissues
Hagiography	Lives of the saints
Halology	Salts
Hamartiology	Doctrine of sin
Helcology	Ulcers
Helminthology	Worms (especially internal worms)
Hemipterology	Hemiptera family (bedbugs, aphids, etc.)
Heparology, hepatology	The liver
Heraldry	Genealogy (especially aristocratic lineage)
Hermeneutics	Interpretation and explanation (especially interpretation of the Bible)
Herniology	Hernias
Herpetology	Reptiles and amphibians
Heterology	Abnormalities of tissue structure
Hippiatrics	Horse diseases (*also called* hippopathology)
Hippology	Horses
Hippopathology	*See* hippiatrics
Histology	Microscopic features of animal and plant tissues
History	Past events, especially human affairs
Horometry	Measuring time
Horticulture	Cultivation of gardens
Hydraulics	Engineering applications of laws applying to water and other liquids in motion
Hydrodynamics	Forces acting on or produced by liquids (*also called* hydromechanics)
Hydrogeology	Water on/below the earth's surface
Hydrokinetics	Laws of gases/liquids in motion
Hydrology	Water on the earth and in the atmosphere

Name	Field of Study
Hydromechanics	*See* hydrodynamics
Hydroponics	Growing plants in special solutions instead of soil
Hydrostatics	Equilibrium and pressure of liquids
Hyetography	Geographical distribution of rainfall
Hygienics	Health and hygiene
Hygrology	Atmospheric humidity
Hymenopterology	Hymenoptera family (bees, wasps, ants, etc.)
Hypnology	Sleep, hypnotism
Hypsography	Land areas above sea level
Hysterology	The uterus
Iamatology	Remedies
Iatrochemistry	Application of chemistry for healing purposes
Ichnology	Fossil footprints
Ichthyology	Fish
Immunogenetics	Immunity with respect to genetic formation
Immunology	Immunity from disease
Insectology	*See* entomology
Isagogics	Biblical writings, emphasizing the literature and cultural history of the Bible
Kinematics	Motion of objects without reference to the external forces which cause the motion
Kinesics	'Body language' or non-verbal gestures of communication (*also called* pasimology)
Kinetics	Motion of objects with reference to the external forces acting on them
Koniology	Atmospheric dust and other airborne pollutants
Lalopathology	Speech disorders
Laryngology	Larynx
Lepidopterology	Butterflies and moths

Name	Field of Study
Lexicology	The form, development and meaning of words
Lichenology	Lichens
Limnology	Ponds, lakes
Linguistics	Language and its structure
Lithology	Mineral composition and structure of rocks
Liturgiology	Church rituals and their symbolism
Logistics	Movement and supply of troops
Macrobiotics	Longevity
Malacology	*See* conchology
Mammalogy	Mammals
Mathematics	Abstract study of number, quantity and space
Mensuration	Science of measurement
Merology	Body fluids and basic tissues
Metaethics	Foundation of ethics
Metalinguistics	Language in its cultural context
Metallurgy	Science of producing, refining and use of metals
Metamathematics	Logical analysis of basic principles of mathematics
Metaphysics	Theoretical study of being and knowing
Meteoritics	*See* astrolithology
Meteorology	Climate and weather variations
Methodology	(1) Application of reason to science and philosophy (2) The science of method (order) and classification
Metoposcopy	*See* physiognomy
Metrology	Science of weights and measures
Miasmology	Fogs, smogs
Microbiology	Micro-organisms
Micrology	Microscopic objects
Mineralogy	Minerals (*also called* oryctology)
Momiology	Mummies

Name	Field of Study
Morphology	(1) Form and structure of animals and plants
	(2) Word formation patterns
Morphonomy	Laws of form in nature
Muscology	Mosses
Mycology	Fungi
Myology	Muscles, musculature
Myrmecology	Ants
Nealogy	Early stages of animal development
Neonatology	The newborn
Neontology	Recently living plants and animals
Neossology	Young birds
Nephology	Clouds
Nephrology	Kidneys
Neurology	Nerves and nerve systems (especially diseases of)
Neuropsychiatry	Diseases of the mind and nervous system
Neuropterology	Neuroptera family (lacewings, etc.)
Nidology	Birds' nests
Noology	Intuition and reason
Obstetrics	Care of women before, during and after childbirth
Oceanography	Oceans, seas
Odontology	Teeth and surrounding tissues
Oenology	Making wines (*also called* viticulture)
Olfactology	Scientific study of the sense of smell
Ombrology	Rainfall
Oncology	Tumours
Oneirology	Science and interpretation of dreams
Onomastics	Names and their origins
Oology	Birds' eggs
Ophiology	Snakes
Ophthalmology	Eyes, eye diseases and defects

Name	Field of Study
Optics	Properties of light (*also called* photology)
Organology	Organs of plants and animals
Ornithology	Birds
Orology	Scientific study of mountains
Orthodontics	Malformed teeth and other oral problems
Orthoepy	Correct pronunciation
Orthography	Correct spelling
Orthology	Correct use of language
Orthopaedics	Bone and muscle deformities
Orthopsychiatry	Prevention of mental/behavioural disorders
Orthopterology	Orthoptera family (cockroaches, grasshoppers, etc.)
Orthoptics	Eye irregularities, especially muscle problems
Oryctology	*See* mineralogy
Osmonosology	Disorders of the sense of smell
Osteology	Bones and diseases of
Otolaryngology	Ear, nose and throat
Otology	Diseases of the ear
Ovology	Formation and structure of animal ova
Paedeutics	Science of learning
Paediatrics	Medical care of infants, children and adolescents
Paedogogics	Science or art of teaching/education
Palaeobiology	Fossil plants and animals
Palaeobotany	Fossil plants
Palaeoecology	Plants, animals and their environment in the distant past
Palaeoethnology	Early man
Palaeogeography	Features of the earth as they existed in past geological ages
Palaeography	Ancient writings
Palaeoichthyology	Fossil fish
Palaeology	Antiquities

Name	Field of Study
Palaeomammalogy	Mammals of past ages
Palaeontology	Life in the geological past
Palaeopedology	Soils of past geological ages
Palaeopathology	Diseases from the distant past
Palaeornithology	Fossil birds
Palaeozoology	Fossil animals
Pantology	Systematic survey of all branches of learning
Parapsychology	Psychic phenomena
Paroemiology	Proverbs
Pasimology	*See* kinesics
Pathognomy	The emotions and signs or expressions of emotion
Pathology	Causes, origin and nature of disease
Pedodontics	Children's dental care
Pedology	(1) Soils
	(2) Physical and psychological events of childhood
Pelycology	Pelvic structure
Penology	(1) Science of the punishment of crime
	(2) Science of the management of prisons
Perastadics	Space flying
Periodontics	Diseases of bone, tissue and gum (mouth)
Petrogenesis	Formation of rocks
Petrology	Origin, structure and composition of rocks
Phaenology	Climate and its effects on living organisms
Pharmacology	Preparation, use, effects and dosage of drugs
Pharyngology	Pharynx
Phenology	Organisms as affected by climate (e.g. migration of birds, blooming of flowers)
Philology	Science of language
Philosophy	Enquiry into truths and knowledge of reality
Phletology	Veins of the body
Phonetics	Vocal sounds (and their classification)

Name	Field of Study
Phorology	Disease carriers, epidemics and endemic diseases
Photics	Light
Photodynamics	Light in relation to the movement of plants
Photology	*See* optics
Phyllotaxy	Arrangement and distribution of leaves
Physics	Interactions of matter and energy
Physiognomy	Determining aspects of character from physical, especially facial, features (*also called* metoposcopy)
Physiography	Physical geography
Physiology	Functions of organisms and their parts
Phytobiology	Plant biology
Phytogeography	Geographical distribution of plants
Phytology	*See* botany
Pistology	Characteristics of faith
Pneumology	Human respiratory system
Polemics	History of ecclesiastical disputes
Pomology	Fruit
Ponerology	Sin, evil and wrong-doing
Potamology	Rivers
Praxeology	Human behaviour and conduct
Proctology	Disorders of rectum and anus
Protozoology	Protozoa (minute invertebrates, e.g. amoeba)
Psephology	Elections
Psychiatry	Study, treatment and prevention of mental illness
Psychodiagnostics	Evaluation of personality
Psycholinguistics	Relationship between language and behaviour patterns
Psychology	The mind and mental processes, emotions and desires
Psychopathology	Causes and nature of mental illness

Name	Field of Study
Psychopharmacology	Drugs that alter emotional and mental conditions
Psychotherapy	Treating psychological disorders using psychological methods
Pteridology	*See* filicology
Pyretology	Fevers
Pyrology	Fire and heat, especially chemical analysis of
Radiogenetics	Effects of radioactivity on genes
Radiology	Radiation for diagnosis and therapy
Rhinology	The nose and its diseases
Robotics	Application of automated machinery to accomplish tasks normally done by hand
Seismography	Measurement of earthquakes
Selenology	Moon
Semantics	Meaning of words (*also called* semasiology, sematology, semology)
Semiotics	Signs
Semitics	Semitic languages and culture
Serology	Serums
Siagonology	Jaw bones
Sindology	Funeral shrouds
Sinology	Chinese culture
Sociology	Origin, development, structure and function of human society
Somatology	Man's physical characteristics
Sophiology	Science of ideas
Speleology	Caves
Sphagnology	Sphagnum mosses
Sphygmology	The pulse
Splanchnology	Viscera (large internal organs of the body)
Spongology	Sponges

Name	Field of Study
Statics	Matter and forces at rest or in equilibrium
Stirpiculture	Selective breeding
Stomatology	Diseases of the mouth
Stratigraphy	Stratified rocks
Sumerology	Sumerian civilization
Syndesmology	Ligaments of the body
Synecology	Relationships of various groups of organisms to a common environment
Syntax	Principles of grammatical sentence construction
Taxonomy	Principles of classification
Tectonics	The earth's crust
Teleology	Ends or final causes with particular reference to evidence of purpose or design in nature
Telmatology	Wetlands, marshes, swamps
Tenology	Tendons
Teratology	Malfunctions in animals and plants
Testaceology	Shell-bearing animals
Thalassography	Areas of water such as gulfs, sounds, etc.
Thanatology	Death and the dead
Thaumatology	Miracles
Theology	Theistic religions (especially Christianity)
Theoretics	Theories and hypotheses (applied to any field of learning)
Thermodynamics	Relationship between heat and other types of energy
Thermogeography	Geographical factors affecting temperature
Thermokinematics	Movement of heat
Thermostatics	Equilibrium of heat
Thremmatology	Breeding of domestic plants and animals
Topology	(1) Characteristics of geometrical figures that remain unaffected by changes in shape or size (2) Plant localities

Name	Field of Study
Toponymy	Place-names of a district
Toxicology	Poisons
Traumatology	Wounds and their treatment
Trichology	Hair and hair diseases
Trigonometry	Relationships of sides and angles of triangles
Trophology	*See* alimentology
Typhlology	Blindness and its prevention
Uranography	Studying and mapping the heavens
Urbanology	Urban problems and conditions
Uredinology	Branch of mycology which studies rusts
Urology	Diseases of the kidney
Venereology	Venereal diseases
Vexillology	Flags, flag design
Virology	Viruses
Viticulture	*See* oenology
Volcanology	Volcanoes
Xylology	Structure of wood
Zenography	Jupiter (planet)
Zoobiology	*See* zoology
Zoogeography	Geographical distribution of animal life (*also called* faunology)
Zoology	All living creatures (*also called* zoobiology)
Zoopathology	Animal diseases
Zoophysiology	Animal physiology
Zoophytology	Zoophytes (animals such as sponges, corals, etc.)
Zoopsychology	Animal behaviour
Zymology	*See* enzymology

PHOBIAS

A phobia is defined as an intense dislike or irrational fear of a given situation or thing. *Phobia* is Greek for 'fear'; Phobos was a Greek god who inspired fear and terror in his enemies.

Phobia	Fear of
ablutophobia	washing (oneself)
acarophobia	mites, ticks
acerophobia	sourness
acoustiphobia	noise
acrophobia	heights
aeronausiphobia	air sickness
aerophobia	(1) fresh air, draughts (2) flying
agiophobia	crossing streets
agoraphobia	open spaces
agraphobia	sexual abuse
agrizoophobia	animals (wild)
aichmophobia	pointed objects
ailurophobia	cats
algophobia	pain
alliumphobia	garlic
allodoxaphobia	opinions (others')
amathophobia	dust
amaxophobia	vehicles (riding on)
amnesiophobia	amnesia
amychophobia	scratched (being)
anablepophobia	high places (looking up at)
androphobia	men
anginaphobia	narrowness
anginophobia	heart attack
Anglophobia	England, English
anklyophobia	immobility (of a joint)
anthophobia	flowers

Phobia	Fear of
anthropophobia	people
anuptaphobia	staying single
apeirophobia	infinity
aphephobia	touching, being touched
apiphobia	bees
arachnophobia	spiders
asthenophobia	weakness
astraphobia	lightning
ataxiophobia	untidiness
atelophobia	imperfection
atephobia	ruin
aurophobia	gold
automysophobia	dirt (on oneself)
autophobia	solitude
bacillophobia	bacteria
ballistophobia	missiles
barophobia	gravity
basiphobia	walking
bathophobia	(1) depth (2) bathing
batophobia	high buildings
batrachophobia	frogs, toads
belonephobia	pins, needles
bibliophobia	books
blennophobia	slime
bogyphobia	demons, goblins
botanophobia	plants
bromhidrosiphobia	body odour
brontophobia	thunder
carcinomophobia	cancer
cardiophobia	heart disease
carnophobia	meat
catapedaphobia	jumping (from both high and low places)

Phobia	Fear of
cathisophobia	sitting still
catoptrophobia	mirrors
Celtophobia	Celts, Celtic
chaetophobia	hair
cheimaphobia	cold
cherophobia	gaiety
chionophobia	snow
cholerophobia	cholera
chorophobia	dancing
chrematophobia	money (touching)
chromophobia	colours
chronophobia	time
cibophobia	food
claustrophobia	locked in (being)
climacophobia	stairs
clinophobia	bed (going to)
clithrophobia	enclosed spaces
cnidophobia	insect stings
coimetrophobia	cemeteries
coitophobia	sexual intercourse
cometophobia	comets
computerphobia	computers
coprophobia	excrement
coprostasophobia	constipation
cremnophobia	steep places
cryophobia	ice, frost
crystallophobia	glass
cyclophobia	bicycles
cymophobia	waves (sea)
cynophobia	dogs
cyprianophobia	prostitutes
cypridophobia	venereal disease

Phobia	Fear of
decidophobia	decisions
defecalgesiophobia	defecation (painful)
deipnophobia	dining, dinner conversation
demonophobia	devils, evil spirits
demophobia	crowds
dentophobia	dentists
dermatophobia	skin
dermatosiophobia	skin disease
dextrophobia	right-hand side of body (objects on)
diabetophobia	diabetes
didaskaleinophobia	school
dikephobia	justice
dinophobia	dizziness
diplopiaphobia	double vision
dipsophobia	alcohol (drinking)
dishabillophobia	undressing (in front of someone)
domatophobia	home (*see also* nostophobia)
doraphobia	fur, animal skin
dysmorphophobia	deformity
dystychiphobia	accidents
electrophobia	electricity
eleutherophobia	freedom
emetophobia	vomiting, emetics
enetophobia	needles
entomophobia	insects
eosophobia	dawn
epistaxiophobia	nosebleeds
ergasiophobia	work
erotophobia	sexual feelings
erythrophobia	(1) red (2) blushing
eurotophobia	female genitals

Phobia	Fear of
Francophobia	France, French
gamophobia	marriage
gelophobia	laughter
genuphobia	knees
gephyrophobia	bridges (crossing)
gerascophobia	ageing
Germanophobia	Germany, Germans
geumophobia	flavours
graphophobia	writing
gymnophobia	nudity
gynaephobia	women
hadephobia	hell
hagiophobia	saints
hamartophobia	sin
harpaxophobia	robbers
hedonophobia	pleasure
heliophobia	sunlight
Hellenologophobia	(1) Greek terms
	(2) complex scientific terms
hemaphobia	blood
herpetophobia	reptiles
hierophobia	sacred objects
hippophobia	horses
hodophobia	travel
homichlophobia	fog
homophobia	homosexuals
hormephobia	shock
hydrophobia	(1) water (2) rabies (*see also* kynophobia)
hygrophobia	dampness
hylephobia	(1) woods (2) materialism
hypengyophobia	responsibility
hypnophobia	sleep

Phobia	Fear of
iatrophobia	doctors
ichthyophobia	fish
ideophobia	ideas
illyngophobia	vertigo
iophobia	(1) poisons (2) rust
isopterophobia	termites
ithyphallophobia	penis (erect)
Japanophobia	Japan, Japanese
Judaeophobia	Jews, Judaism
kakorrhaphiophobia	failure
katagelophobia	ridicule
kenophobia	empty rooms
keraunophobia	thunder and lightning
kinesophobia	motion
kleptophobia	thieves
koinoniphobia	crowded rooms
kopophobia	fatigue
kynophobia	pseudo-rabies (see also hydrophobia)
lachanophobia	vegetables
laliophobia	talking
lepraphobia	leprosy
leukophobia	white
levophobia	left-hand side of the body (objects on)
lilapsophobia	hurricanes
limnophobia	lakes
logophobia	words
lyssophobia	insanity
macrophobia	long waits
maniaphobia	madness (*see also* lyssophobia)
mechanophobia	machinery

Phobia	Fear of
medectophobia	penis (contour of, visible through clothes)
megalophobia	large objects
meningitophobia	meningitis
menophobia	menstruation
merinthophobia	bound (being)
metallophobia	metal
meterorophobia	meteors
methyphobia	alcohol
microbiophobia	microbes
mnemophobia	memories
molysomophobia	infection
monopathophobia	disease (a particular)
motorphobia	motor vehicles
musicophobia	music
musophobia	mice
myrmecophobia	ants
mysophobia	dirt
mythophobia	(1) lying (2) stories and myths
necrophobia	death, corpses
negrophobia	Negroes
neopharmaphobia	drugs (new)
nephophobia	clouds
noctiphobia	night
nosocomephobia	hospitals
nosophobia	disease
nostophobia	home (returning to) (see also domatophobia)
nucleomitophobia	atomic energy
nyctophobia	darkness
obesophobia	fat (becoming)
odontophobia	teeth
oenophobia	wine
olfactophobia	smells

Phobia	Fear of
ombrophobia	rain
ommatophobia	eyes
oneirogmophobia	wet dreams
oneirophobia	dreams
onomatophobia	a particular name or word
ophidiophobia	snakes
optophobia	eyes (opening one's)
ornithophobia	birds
ostraconophobia	shellfish
panophobia	everything
papaphobia	pope
papyrophobia	paper
paralipophobia	duty (neglect of)
parasitophobia	parasites
parthenophobia	girls (young)
pathophobia	disease, illness
patriophobia	hereditary disease
peccatiphobia	wrongdoing
pediculophobia	lice
pedophobia	dolls
peladophobia	baldness
peniaphobia	poverty
pentheraphobia	mother-in-law
phagophobia	swallowing
pharmacophobia	drugs
phasmophobia	ghosts
phengophobia	daylight
philemaphobia	kissing
philophobia	love
philosophobia	philosophy, philosophers
phobophobia	fear
phonophobia	speaking aloud
photaugiophobia	lights (glaring)

Phobia	Fear of
photophobia	light
phronemophobia	thinking
phthisiophobia	tuberculosis
placophobia	tombstones
pnigophobia	choking
pogonophobia	beards
poinephobia	punishment
politicophobia	politicians
porphyrophobia	purple
potamophobia	rivers
potophobia	drink (usually alcohol)
primeisodophobia	virginity (losing one's)
proctophobia	rectal disease
prosophobia	progress
psellismophobia	stuttering
psychophobia	mind
pteronophobia	feathers
pyrexiphobia	fever
pyrophobia	fire
radiophobia	X-rays, radiation
rhabdophobia	(1) being beaten (2) magic
rhypophobia	filth
rhytiphobia	wrinkles (gettings)
Russophobia	Russia, Russians
Satanophobia	Satan
scelerophobia	attack
sciophobia	shadows
scoleciphobia	worms
scopophobia	looked at (being)
selaphobia	light (flashes of)
selenophobia	moon
septophobia	decaying matter

Phobia	Fear of
sexophobia	opposite sex
siderodromophobia	railways
siderophobia	stars
Sinophobia	China, Chinese
Slavophobia	Slavs, Slavic
soceraphobia	parents-in-law
sophophobia	learning
spacephobia	outer space
spectrophobia	spectres
spermatophobia	semen
stasibasiphobia	standing and walking
stasiphobia	standing
staurophobia	crucifixes
symbolophobia	symbols
syngenesophobia	relatives
syphiliphobia	syphilis
tabophobia	wasting sickness
tachophobia	speed
taeniophobia	tapeworms
taphephobia	buried alive (being)
tapinophobia	small objects
taurophobia	bulls
technophobia	technology
telephonophobia	telephones
teletophobia	religious ceremonies
teratophobia	monsters (or giving birth to a monster)
testophobia	taking tests
tetanophobia	tetanus (lockjaw)
textophobia	fabrics (particular)
thasaophobia	sitting down
thaasophobia	sea
theatrophobia	theatres
theologicophobia	theology

Phobia	Fear of
theophobia	God
thermophobia	heat
tocophobia	childbirth
tomophobia	surgery
topophobia	(1) certain places
	(2) performing (stagefright)
toxiphobia	poisoned (being)
traumatophobia	(1) injury (physical) (2) war
tremophobia	trembling
trichinophobia	hair disease
triskaidekaphobia	thirteen
tropophobia	changes (making)
trypanophobia	injections
uranophobia	heavens
urophobia	urinating
vaccinophobia	vaccination
venustaphobia	beautiful women
vestiophobia	clothes
xenophobia	foreigners
xerophobia	dryness
zelophobia	jealousy
zoophobia	animals

Fear of	Phobia
accidents	dystychiphobia
ageing	gerascophobia
air sickness	aeronausiphobia
air (fresh), draughts	aerophobia (see also flying)
alcohol	methyphobia
alcohol (drinking)	dipsophobia

Fear of	Phobia
amnesia	amnesiophobia
animals	zoophobia
animals (wild)	agrizoophobia
animal skin, fur	doraphobia
ants	myrmecophobia
atomic energy	nucleomitophobia
attack	scelerophobia
auroral lights	auroraphobia
bacteria	bacillophobia
baldness	peladophobia
bathing	bathophobia (*see also* depth)
beards	pogonophobia
beaten (being)	rhabdophobia (*see also* magic)
bed (going to)	clinophobia
bees	apiphobia
bicycles	cyclophobia
birds	ornithophobia
blood	hemaphobia
blushing	erythrophobia (*see also* red)
body odour	bromhidrosiphobia
books	bibliophobia
bound (being)	merinthophobia
bridges (crossing)	gephyrophobia
buildings (high)	batophobia
bulls	taurophobia
buried alive (being)	taphephobia
cancer	carcinomophobia
cats	ailurophobia
Celts, Celtic	Celtophobia
cemeteries	coimetrophobia
certain places	topophobia (*see also* performing)
changes (making)	tropophobia

Fear of	Phobia
childbirth	tocophobia
China, Chinese	Sinophobia
choking	pnigophobia
cholera	cholerophobia
clothes	vestiophobia
clouds	nephophobia
cold	cheimaphobia
colours	chromophobia
comets	cometophobia
complex scientific (or Greek) terms	Hellenologophobia
computers	computerphobia
constipation	coprostasophobia
corpses, death	necrophobia
crossing streets	agiophobia
crowded rooms	koinoniphobia
crowds	demophobia
crucifixes	staurophobia
dampness	hygrophobia
dancing	chorophobia
darkness	nyctophobia
dawn	eosophobia
daylight	phengophobia
death, corpses	necrophobia
decaying matter	septophobia
decisions	decidophobia
defecation (painful)	defecalgesiophobia
deformity	dysmorphophobia
demons, goblins	bogyphobia
dentists	dentophobia
depth	bathophobia (see also bathing)
devils, evil spirits	demonophobia
diabetes	diabetophobia

Fear of	Phobia
dining, dinner conversation	deipnophobia
dirt	mysophobia
dirt (on oneself)	automysophobia
disease	nosophobia
disease (hereditary)	patriophobia
disease, illness	pathophobia
disease (particular)	monopathophobia
disease (rectal)	proctophobia
disease (skin)	dermatosiophobia
dizziness	dinophobia
doctors	iatrophobia
dogs	cynophobia
dolls	pedophobia
double vision	diplopiaphobia
draughts, fresh air	aerophobia (*see also* flying)
draughts, winds	anemophobia
dreams	oneirophobia
dreams (wet)	oneirogmophobia
drink (usually alcohol)	potophobia
drugs	pharmacophobia
drugs (new)	neopharmaphobia
dryness	xerophobia
dust	amathophobia
duty (neglect of)	paralipophobia
electricity	electrophobia
emetics, vomiting	emetophobia
empty rooms	kenophobia
enclosed spaces	clithrophobia
England, English	Anglophobia
everything	panophobia
evil spirits, devils	demonophobia
excrement	coprophobia
eyes	ommatophobia

Fear of	**Phobia**
eyes (opening one's)	optophobia
fabrics (particular)	textophobia
failure	kakorrhaphiophobia
fat (becoming)	obesophobia
fatigue	kopophobia
fear	phobophobia
feathers	pteronophobia
fever	pyrexiphobia
filth	rhypophobia
fire	pyrophobia
fish	ichthyophobia
flashes of light	selaphobia
flavours	geumophobia
flowers	anthophobia
flying	aerophobia (*see also* air (fresh), draughts)
fog	homichlophobia
food	cibophobia
foreigners	xenophobia
France, French	Francophobia
freedom	eleutherophobia
fresh air, draughts	aerophobia (*see also* flying)
frogs, toads	batrachophobia
frost, ice	cryophobia
fur, animal skin	doraphobia
gaiety	cherophobia
garlic	alliumphobia
genitals (female)	eurotophobia
Germany, Germans	Germanophobia
ghosts	phasmophobia
girls (young)	parthenophobia
glass	crystallophobia

Fear of	Phobia
goblins, demons	bogyphobia
God	theophobia
gold	aurophobia
gravity	barophobia
Greek (or complex scientific) terms	Hellenologophobia
hair	chaetophobia
hair disease	trichinophobia
heart attack	angionophobia
heart disease	cardiophobia
heat	thermophobia
heavens	uranophobia
heights	acrophobia
hell	hadephobia
high buildings	batophobia
high places (looking up at)	anablepophobia
home	domatophobia
home (returning to)	nostophobia
homosexuals	homophobia
horses	hippophobia
hospitals	nosocomephobia
hurricanes	lilapsophobia
ice, frost	cryophobia
ideas	ideophobia
illness, disease	pathophobia
immobility (of a joint)	ankylophobia
imperfection	atelophobia
infection	molysomophobia
infinity	apeirophobia
injections	trypanophobia
injury (physical)	traumatophobia (*see also* war)
insanity	lyssophobia (*see also* madness)

Fear of	Phobia
insects	entomophobia
insect stings	cnidophobia
Japan, Japanese	Japanophobia
jealousy	zelophobia
Jews, Judaism	Judaeophobia
jumping (from both high and low places)	catapedaphobia
justice	dikephobia
kissing	philemaphobia
knees	genuphobia
lakes	limnophobia
large objects	megalophobia
laughter	gelophobia
learning	sophophobia
left hand side of the body (objects on)	levophobia
leprosy	lepraphobia
lice	pediculophobia
light	photophobia
light (flashes of)	selaphobia
lightning	astraphobia
lights (glaring)	photaugiophobia
locked in (being)	claustrophobia
long waits	macrophobia
looked at (being)	scopophobia
love	philophobia
lying, myths and stories	mythophobia
machinery	mechanophobia
madness	maniaphobia *(see also* insanity)
magic	rhabdophobia (*see also* beaten, being)

Fear of	Phobia
making changes	tropophobia
marriage	gamophobia
materialism	hylephobia (*see also* woods)
meat	carnophobia
memories	mnemophobia
men	androphobia
meningitis	meningitophobia
menstruation	menophobia
metal	metallophobia
meteors	meteorophobia
mice	musophobia
microbes	microbiophobia
mind	psychophobia
mirrors	catoptrophobia
missiles	ballistophobia
mites, ticks	acarophobia
money (touching)	chrematophobia
monsters (or giving birth to a monster)	teratophobia
moon	selenophobia
mother-in-law	pentheraphobia
motion	kinesophobia
motor vehicles	motorphobia
music	musicophobia
myths, stories and lying	mythophobia
name (a particular name or word)	onomatophobia
narrowness	anginaphobia
needles	enetophobia
needles, pins	belonephobia
Negroes	negrophobia
night	noctiphobia
noise	acoustiphobia

Fear of	Phobia
nosebleeds	epistaxiophobia
novelty	cainophobia
nudity	gymnophobia
objects (large)	megalophobia
objects (pointed)	aichmophobia
objects (sacred)	hierophobia
objects (small)	tapinophobia
open spaces	agoraphobia
opinions (others')	allodoxaphobia
opposite sex	sexophobia
outer space	spacephobia
pain	algophobia
paper	papyrophobia
parasites	parasitophobia
parents-in-law	soceraphobia
penis (contour of, visible through clothes)	medectophobia
penis (erect)	ithyphallophobia
people	anthropophobia
performing (stagefright)	topophobia (*see also* places (certain))
philosophy, philosophers	philosophobia
physical injury	traumatophobia (*see also* war)
pins, needles	belonephobia
places (certain)	topophobia (see also performing)
places (steep)	cremnophobia
plants	botanophobia
pleasure	hedonophobia
pointed obects	aichmophobia
poisoned (being)	toxiphobia
poisons	iophobia (*see also* rust)
politicians	politicophobia
pope	papaphobia

Fear of	Phobia
poverty	peniaphobia
progress	prosophobia
prostitutes	cyprianophobia
pseudo-rabies	kynophobia (*see also* rabies)
punishment	poinephobia
purple	porphyrophobia
rabies	hydrophobia (*see also* pseudo-rabies)
radiation, X-rays	radiophobia
railways	siderodromophobia
rain	ombrophobia
red	erythrophobia (*see also* blushing)
relatives	syngenesophobia
religious ceremonies	teletophobia
reptiles	herpetophobia
responsibility	hypengyophobia
ridicule	katagelophobia
riding in vehicles	amaxophobia
right-hand side of the body (objects on)	dextrophobia
rivers	potamophobia
robbers	harpaxophobia
rooms (empty)	kenophobia
rooms (crowded)	koinoniphobia
ruin	atephobia
Russia, Russian	Russophobia
rust	iophobia (*see also* poisons)
sacred objects	hierophobia
saints	hagiophobia
Satan	Satanophobia
school	didaskaleinophobia
scientific terms (complex) or Greek terms	Hellenologophobia

Fear of	Phobia
scratched (being)	amychophobia
sea	thalassophobia
semen	spermatophobia
sex, opposite	sexophobia
sexual abuse	agraphobia
sexual feelings	erotophobia
sexual intercourse	coitophobia
shadows	sciophobia
shellfish	ostraconophobia
shock	hormephobia
sin	hamartophobia
single, staying	anuptaphobia
sitting down	thaasophobia
sitting still	cathisophobia
skin	dermatophobia
skin disease	dermatosiophobia
Slavs, Slavic	Slavophobia
sleep	hypnophobia
slime	blennophobia
small objects	tapinophobia
smells	olfactophobia
snakes	ophidiophobia
snow	chionophobia
solitude	autophobia
sourness	acerophobia
space (outer)	spacephobia
spaces (enclosed)	clithrophobia
spaces (open)	agoraphobia
speaking aloud	phonophobia
spectres	spectrophobia
speed	tachophobia
spiders	arachnophobia
stage fright	topophobia (*see also* places (certain))
stairs	climacophobia

Fear of	Phobia
standing	stasiphobia
standing and walking	stasibasiphobia
stars	siderophobia
staying single	anuptaphobia
stories, myths and lying	mythophobia
streets (crossing)	agiophobia
stuttering	psellismophobia
sunlight	heliophobia
surgery	tomophobia
swallowing	phagophobia
symbols	symbolophobia
syphilis	syphiliphobia
taking tests	testophobia
talking	laliophobia
tapeworms	taeniophobia
technology	technophobia
teeth	odontophobia
teleology	teleophobia
telephones	telephonophobia
termites	isopterophobia
tests, taking	testophobia
tetanus (lockjaw)	tetanophobia
theatres	theatrophobia
theology	theologicophobia
thieves	kleptophobia
thinking	phronemophobia
thirteen	triskaidekaphobia
thunder	brontophobia
thunder and lightning	keraunophobia
ticks, mites	acarophobia
time	chronophobia
toads, frogs	batrachophobia
tombstones	placophobia

Fear of	Phobia
touching, being touched	aphephobia
touching money	chrematophobia
travel	hodophobia
trembling	tremophobia
tuberculosis	phthisiophobia
tyrants	tyrannophobia
undressing (in front of someone)	dishabillophobia
untidiness	ataxiophobia
urinating	urophobia
vaccination, vaccines	vaccinophobia
vegetables	lachanophobia
vehicles, riding in	amaxophobia
venereal disease	cypridophobia
vertigo	illyngophobia
virginity, losing one's	primeisodophobia
vomiting, emetics	emetophobia
walking	basiphobia
walking and standing	stasibasiphobia
war	traumatophobia (*see also* injury (physical))
washing oneself	ablutophobia
wasting sickness	tabophobia
water	hydrophobia
waves (sea)	cymophobia
weakness	asthenophobia
wet dreams	oneirogmophobia
white	leukophobia
wine	oenophobia
women	gynaephobia

Fear of	Phobia
women (beautiful)	venustaphobia
woods	hylephobia (*see also* materialism)
word (a particular word or name)	onomatophobia
words	logophobia
work	ergasiophobia
worms	scoleciphobia
wrinkles (getting)	rhytiphobia
writing	graphophobia
wrongdoing	peccatiphobia
X-rays, radiation	radiophobia
young girls	parthenophobia

COLLECTIVE NOUNS

Noun	Collective term
actors	company
antelopes	herd
bears	sleuth
bees	swarm or grist
birds	flock, flight or congregation
bishops	bench
buffaloes	herd
cattle	herd or drove
chickens	brood
cranes	herd, sedge or siege
cubs	litter
curlews	herd
deer	herd
directors	board
doves	flight or dule
ducks	team or padding
eggs	clutch

Noun	Collective term
fish	catch
fish	shoal or run
flies	swarm or grist
flowers	bouquet
geese	flock, gaggle or skein
giraffes	herd
gnats	swarm or cloud
goats	herd or tribe
grouse	brood, covey or pack
gulls	colony
hares	down or husk
hens	brood
herons	sedge or siege
herrings	shoal or glean
horses	herd or drove
hounds	pack, mute or cry
insects	swarm
judges	bench
kangaroos	troop
leopards	leap
lions	pride or troop
mares	stud
monkeys	troop
oxen	yoke, drove, team or herd
partridges	covey
people	audience, crowd, congregation or mob
pigeons	flock or flight
pigs	litter
plovers	stand or wing
policemen	posse
ponies	herd
porpoises	school or gam
poultry	run
prisoners	gang

Noun	Collective term
pups	litter
quails	bevy
rabbits	nest
racehorses	string or field
rooks	building or clamour
sailors	crew
seals	herd, pod or rookery
sheep	flock
ships	fleet
sparrows	host
stories	anthology
swallows	flight
swans	herd or bevy
swifts	flock
swine	herd, sounder or dryft
thieves	gang
whales	school or run
wolves	pack, rout or herd
workmen	gang

COLLECTORS AND ENTHUSIASTS

Name	Area of Interest
Aerophilatelist	Airmail stamps
Ailurophile	Cats
Antiquary	Antiquities
Antivivisectionist	Campaign against vivisection
Arachnologist	Spiders
Arctophile	Teddy bears
Argyrothecologist	Money boxes
Audiophile	Reproduction of sound, especially music recordings, broadcasts
Balletomane	Ballet
Baptisaphily	Christian names
Bibliolatrist	Excessive devotion to books

Name	Area of Interest
Bibliomane	Collecting books
Bibliopegist	Bookbinding
Bibliophile	Book-lover
Brandophily	Cigar bands
Cagophily	Keys
Campanologist	Bell-ringing
Canophilist, cynophilist	Dogs
Cartophily	Cigarette and chewing-gum cards
Coleopterist	Beetles
Conchology	Shells
Conservationist	Conservation, esp. of natural resources
Copoclephily	Key-rings with advertisements
Cruciverbamorist	Crossword puzzles
Cumyxaphily	Matchboxes
Dantophilist	Works of Dante
Deltiology	Picture postcards
Ecclesiologist	Church building and decoration
Egger	Birds' eggs
Entomologist	Insects
Environmentalist	Preservation of the environment
Ephemerist	Diary- or journal-keeping
Epicure	Refined taste for the pleasures of the table
Errinophily	Stamps (except postage stamps)
Ex-librist	Book-plates
Fusilatelist	Phonecards
Gastronome	Good eating
Gemmologist	Gems
Gourmet	Connoisseur of food and drink
Herpetologist	Reptiles
Hippophile	Horses
Hostelaphily	Outdoor signs from pubs
Iconophilist	Engravings, pictures, prints, etc.
Incunabulist	Early printed books
Labeorphily	Beer-bottle labels

Name	Area of Interest
Laclabphily	Cheese labels
Lepidopterist	Butterflies, moths
Medallist	Medals
Monarchist	Monarchy
Myrmecologist	Ants
Notaphilist	Banknotes
Numismatist	Coins, medals
Oenophile	Wine-lover
Omnibology	Buses
Ophiophilist	Snakes
Orchidophilist	Orchids
Ornithologist	Birds
Orthoepist	Correct pronunciation of words
Orthographist	Correct or proper spelling
Paragrammatist	Paragrams
Paroemographer	Proverbs
Peridromophily	Transport tickets
Philanthropist	Promoting the welfare of mankind
Philatelist	Postage stamps
Phillumeny	Matchbox labels, matchbook covers
Philology	Learning, literature
Philometry	Envelopes with postmarks
Phonophily	Gramophone records
Plangonology	Dolls
Pteridophilist	Ferns
Scripophile	Old bond and share certificates
Sericulturist	Silkworms
Speleologist	Caves
Steganographist	Secret writing, cryptography
Stegophilist	Climbing buildings
Tegestologist	Cardboard beer-mats
Tyrosemiophily	Camembert cheese labels
Ufologist	UFOs
Vexillologist	Flags, banners

Area of Interest	Name
Antiquities	Antiquary
Ants	Myrmecologist
Ballet	Balletomane
Banknotes	Notaphilist
Banners, flags	Vexillologist
Beer-bottle labels	Labeorphily
Beer-mats, cardboard	Tegestologist
Beetles	Coleopterist
Bell-ringing	Campanologist
Birds	Ornithologist
Birds' eggs	Egger
Bond and share certificates, old	Scripophile
Bookbinding	Bibliopegist
Book-lover	Bibliophile
Book-plates	Ex-librist
Books, collecting	Bibliomane
Books, early printed	Incunabulist
Books, excesssive devotion to	Bibliolatrist
Buildings, climbing	Stegophilist
Buses	Omnibology
Butterflies, moths	Lepidopterist
Camembert cheese labels	Tyrosemiophily
Cats	Ailurophile
Caves	Speleologist
Cheese labels	Laclabphily
Chewing-gum and cigarette cards	Cartophily
Christian names	Baptisaphily
Church building and decoration	Ecclesiologist
Cigar bands	Brandophily
Cigarette and chewing-gum cards	Cartophily
Climbing buildings	Stegophilist
Coins, medals	Numismatist
Conservation, esp. of natural resources	Conservationist

Area of Interest	Name
Covers, matchbox, matchbox labels	Phillumeny
Crossword puzzles	Cruciverbamorist
Cryptography, secret writing	Steganographist
Dante, works of	Dantophilist
Diary- or journal-keeping	Ephemerist
Dogs	Canophilist or cynophilist
Dolls	Plangonology
Early printed books	Incunabulist
Eating, good	Gastronome
Engravings, pictures, prints, etc.	Iconophilist
Envelopes with postmarks	Philometry
Environment, preservation of	Environmentalist
Ferns	Pteridophilist
Flags, banners	Vexillologist
Food and drink, connoisseur of	Gourmet
Gems	Gemmologist
Gramophone records	Phonophily
Horses	Hippophile
Insects	Entomologist
Journal- or diary-keeping	Ephemerist
Key-rings with advertisements	Copoclephily
Keys	Cagophily
Labels, beer-bottle	Labeorphily
Labels, Camembert cheese	Tyrosemiophily
Labels, cheese	Laclabphily
Labels, matchbox, matchbook covers	Phillumeny
Learning, literature	Philology
Mankind, promoting the welfare of	Philanthropist
Matchbook covers, matchbox labels	Phillumeny
Matchboxes	Cumyxaphily
Matchbox labels, matchbook covers	Phillumeny
Medals	Medallist
Medals, coins	Numismatist
Monarchy	Monarchist

Area of Interest	Name
Money boxes	Argyrothecologist
Moths, butterflies	Lepidopterist
Names, Christian	Baptisaphily
Orchids	Orchidophilist
Paragrams	Paragrammatist
Phonecards	Fusilatelist
Pictures, prints, engravings, etc.	Iconophilist
Postcards, picture	Deltiology
Postmarks on envelopes	Philometry
Prints, pictures, engravings, etc.	Iconophilist
Proverbs	Paroemographer
Records, gramophone	Phonophily
Reptiles	Herpetologist
Secret writing, cryptography	Steganographist
Share and bond certificates, old	Scripophile
Shells	Conchology
Signs, outdoor, from pubs	Hostelaphily
Silkworms	Sericulturist
Snakes	Ophiophilist
Sound, reproduction of (esp. music recordings, broadcasts)	Audiophile
Spelling, correct or proper	Orthographist
Spiders	Arachnologist
Stamps, airmail	Aerophilatelist
Stamps (except postage stamps)	Errinophile
Stamps, postage	Philatelist
Table, refined taste for pleasures of the	Epicure
Teddy bears	Arctophile
Tickets, transport	Peridromophily
UFOs	Ufologist
Vivisection, campaign against	Antivivisectionist
Welfare of mankind, promoting the	Philanthropist
Wine-lover	Oenophile
Words, correct pronunciation of	Orthoepist

-ARCHIES AND -OCRACIES

Anarchy	Without law
Aristocracy	Privileged order
Autarchy	Economically self-sufficient country
Autocracy	One man absolute rule
Bureaucracy	Officials
Democracy	The people
Despotocracy	A tyrant
Diarchy	Two rulers
Ergatocracy	The workers
Ethnocracy	Race or ethnic group
Gerontocracy	Old men
Gynarchy	Women
Gynaecocracy	Women
Gynocracy	Women
Hierocracy	Priests
Isocracy	All with equal power
Kakistocracy	The worst
Matriarchy	A mother (or mothers)
Meritocracy	In power on ability
Mobocracy	A mob
Monarchy	Hereditary head of state
Monocracy	One person
Ochlocracy	The mob
Oligarchy	Small exclusive class
Pantisocracy	All with equal power
Patriarchy	Male head of family
Plutocracy	The wealthy
Stratocracy	The military
Technocracy	Technical experts
Thearchy	God or gods
Theocracy	Divine guidance
Triarchy	Three people

Sport

OLYMPIC GAMES VENUES

I	1896	Athens, Greece
II	1900	Paris, France
III	1904	St Louis, USA
IV	1908	London, UK
V	1912	Stockholm, Sweden
VI	Allocated to Berlin *(not held)*	
VII	1920	Antwerp, Belgium
VIII	1924	Paris, France
IX	1928	Amsterdam, The Netherlands
X	1932	Los Angeles, USA
XI	1936	Berlin, Germany
XII	Allocated to Tokyo, then Helsinki *(not held)*	
XIII	Allocated to London *(not held)*	
XIV	1948	London, UK
XV	1952	Helsinki, Finland
XVI	1956	Melbourne, Australia
XVII	1960	Rome, Italy
XVIII	1964	Tokyo, Japan
XIX	1968	Mexico City, Mexico
XX	1972	Munich, FRG
XXI	1976	Montreal, Canada
XXII	1980	Moscow, USSR
XXIII	1984	Los Angeles, USA
XXIV	1988	Seoul, South Korea
XXV	1992	Barcelona, Spain
XXVI	1996	Atlanta, USA
XXVII	2000	Sydney, Australia

WINTER OLYMPIC GAMES VENUES

I	1924	Chamonix, France
II	1928	St Moritz, Switzerland
III	1932	Lake Placid, USA
IV	1936	Garmisch-Partenkirchen, Germany
	1940	Games allocated to Sapporo, then St Moritz, then Garmisch-Partenkirchen *(not held)*
	1944	Games allocated to Cortina *(not held)*
V	1948	St Moritz, Switzerland
VI	1952	Oslo, Norway
VII	1956	Cortina, Italy
VIII	1960	Squaw Valley, USA
IX	1964	Innsbruck, Austria
X	1968	Grenoble, France
XI	1972	Sapporo, Japan
XII	1976	Innsbruck, Austria
XIII	1980	Lake Placid, USA
XIV	1984	Sarajevo, Yugoslavia
XV	1988	Calgary, Canada
XVI	1992	Albertville, France
XVII	1994	Lillehammer, Norway*
XVIII	1998	Nagano, Japan
XIX	2002	Salt Lake City, USA

* The two-year gap between Winter Olympics was introduced so that in the future there will be an Olympic games every two years, rather than both Winter and Summer Olympics occurring in the same year every four years.

COMMONWEALTH GAMES VENUES

The title has changed four times.

British Empire Games

I	1930	Hamilton, Canada
II	1934	London, England
III	1938	Sydney, Australia
IV	1950	Auckland, New Zealand

British Empire and Commonwealth Games

V	1954	Vancouver, Canada
VI	1958	Cardiff, Wales
VII	1962	Perth, Australia
VIII	1966	Kingston, Jamaica

British Commonwealth Games

IX	1970	Edinburgh, Scotland
X	1974	Christchurch, New Zealand

Commonwealth Games

XI	1978	Edmonton, Canada
XII	1982	Brisbane, Australia
XIII	1986	Edinburgh, Scotland
XIV	1990	Auckland, New Zealand
XV	1994	Victoria, Canada
XVI	1998	Kuala Lumpur, Malaysia

FOOTBALL WORLD CUP VENUES

1930	Uruguay	1962	Chile	1986	Mexico
1934	Italy	1966	England	1990	Italy
1938	France	1970	Mexico	1994	USA
1950	Brazil	1974	W Germany	1998	France
1954	Switzerland	1978	Argentina		
1958	Sweden	1982	Spain		

FOOTBALL

	FA Cup	Scottish FA Cup	Football League Cup
1988	Wimbledon	Celtic	Luton Town
1989	Liverpool	Celtic	Nottingham Forest
1990	Manchester United	Aberdeen	Nottingham Forest
1991	Tottenham Hotspur	Motherwell	Sheffield Wednesday
1992	Liverpool	Rangers	Manchester United
1993	Arsenal	Rangers	Arsenal
1994	Manchester United	Dundee United	Aston Villa
1995	Everton	Celtic	Liverpool

	Scottish League Cup	Football League	Scottish League
1988	Rangers	Liverpool	Celtic
1989	Rangers	Arsenal	Rangers
1990	Aberdeen	Liverpool	Rangers
1991	Rangers	Arsenal	Rangers
1992	Hibernian	Leeds United	Rangers
1993	Rangers	Manchester United	Rangers
1994	Rangers	Manchester United	Rangers
1995	Raith Rovers	Blackburn Rovers	Rangers

	European Cup	Cup Winners' Cup	UEFA Cup
1988	PSV Eindhoven	Mechelen	Bayer Leverkusen
1989	AC Milan	Barcelona	Napoli
1990	AC Milan	Sampdoria	Juventus
1991	Red Star Belgrade	Manchester United	Inter Milan
1992	Barcelona	Werder Bremen	Ajax Amsterdam
1993	Marseille	AC Parma	Juventus
1994	AC Milan	Arsenal	Inter Milan
1995	Ajax Amsterdam	Real Zaragoza	Parma

	World Cup		**Olympics**
1974	W Germany	1976	GDR
1978	Argentina	1980	Czechoslovakia
1982	Italy	1984	France
1986	Argentina	1988	USSR
1990	W Germany	1992	Spain
1994	Brazil		

CRICKET

	County Champions	**Nat West Trophy**
1988	Worcestershire	Middlesex
1989	Worcestershire	Warwickshire
1990	Middlesex	Lancashire
1991	Essex	Hampshire
1992	Essex	Northamptonshire
1993	Middlesex	Warwickshire
1994	Warwickshire	Worcestershire
1995	Warwickshire	Warwickshire

	Sunday League	**Benson & Hedges**
1988	Worcestershire	Hampshire
1989	Lancashire	Nottinghamshire
1990	Derbyshire	Lancashire
1991	Nottinghamshire	Worcestershire
1992	Middlesex	Hampshire
1993	Glamorgan	Derbyshire
1994	Warwickshire	Warwickshire
1995	Kent	Lancashire

RUGBY

	International	CIS Insurance County	Courage English
1988	France/Wales	Lancashire	
1989	France	Durham	Bath
1990	Scotland	Lancashire	Wasps
1991	England	Cornwall	Bath
1992	England	Lancashire	Bath
1993	France	Lancashire	Bath
1994	Wales	Yorkshire	Bath
1995	England	Warwickshire	Leicester

	Schweppes Welsh	McEwens Scottish	Pilkington Cup
1988	Llanelli	Kelso	Harlequins
1989	Neath	Kelso	Bath
1990	Neath	Melrose	Bath
1991	Llanelli	Boroughmuir	Harlequins
1992	Llanelli	Melrose	Bath
1993	Llanelli	Melrose	Leicester
1994	Cardiff	Melrose	Bath
1995	Swansea	Stirling County	Bath

GOLF

	Open	World Matchplay	PGA
1988	S Ballesteros (Spa)	S Lyle (GB)	I Woosnam (GB)
1989	M Calcavecchia (US)	N Faldo (GB)	N Faldo (GB)
1990	N Faldo (GB)	I Woosnam (GB)	M Harwood (Aus)
1991	I Baker-Finch (Aus)	S Ballesteros (Spa)	S Ballesteros (Spa)
1992	N Faldo (GB)	N Faldo (GB)	T Johnstone (Zim)
1993	G Norman (Aus)	C Pavin (US)	B Langer (Ger)
1994	N Price (Zim)	E. Els (S Afr)	J M Olazabal (Spa)
1995	J Daly (US)	E. Els (S Afr)	B Langer (Ger)

	US Open	US Masters	US PGA
1988	C Strange (US)	S Lyle (GB)	J Sluman (US)
1989	C Strange (US)	N Faldo (GB)	P Stewart (US)
1990	H Irwin (US)	N Faldo (GB)	W Grady (Aus)
1991	P Stewart (US)	I Woosnam (GB)	J Daly (US)
1992	T Kite (US)	F Couples (US)	N Price (Zim)
1993	L Janzen (US)	B Langer (Ger)	P Azinger (US)
1994	E Els (SA)	J M Olazabal (Spa)	N Price (US)
1995	C Pavin (US)	Ben Crenshaw (US)	S Elkington (Aus)

	Ryder Cup	Walker Cup	Curtis Cup
1985	Europe	US	
1986			GB & Ireland
1987	Europe	US	
1988			GB & Ireland
1989	Draw	GB & Ireland	
1990			US
1991	US	US	
1992			GB & Ireland
1993	US	US	
1994			GB & Ireland
1995	Europe	GB & Ireland	

TENNIS
WIMBLEDON

	Men's Singles	Women's Singles	Men's Doubles
1988	S Edberg (Swe)	S Graf (FRG)	K Flach/R Seguso (US)
1989	B Becker (Ger)	S Graf (FRG)	J Fitzgerald (Aus)/ A Jarryd (Swe)
1990	S Edberg (Swe)	M Navratilova (US)	R Leach/J Pugh (US)
1991	M Stich (Ger)	S Graf (Ger)	J Fitzgerald (Aus)/ A Jarryd (Swe)
1992	A Agassi (US)	S Graf (Ger)	J McEnroe (US)/ M Stich (Ger)
1993	P Sampras (US)	S Graf (Ger)	T Woodbridge/ M Woodforde (Aus)
1994	P Sampras (US)	C Martinez (Spa)	T Woodbridge/ M Woodforde (Aus)
1995	P Sampras (US)	S Graf (Ger)	T Woodbridge/ M Woodforde (Aus)

	Women's Doubles	Mixed Doubles
1988	S Graf (FRG)/G Sabatini (Arg)	S Stewart/Z Garrison (US)
1989	J Novotna/H Sukova (Cz)	J Pugh (US)/J Novotna (Cz)
1990	J Novotna/H Sukova (Cz)	R Leach/Z Garrison (US)
1991	L Savchenko/N Zvereva (USSR)	J Fitzgerald/L Smylie (Aus)
1992	G Fernandez (US) /N Zvereva (CIS)	L Savchenko-Neiland (Lat)/ C Suk (Cz)
1993	G Fernandez (US)/N Zvereva (Belarus)	M Navratilova (US)/ M Woodforde (Aus)
1994	G Fernandez (US)/N Zvereva (Belarus)	T Woodbridge (Aus)/ H Sukova (Cz Rep)
1995	A Sanchez-Vicario (Spa)/ J Novotna (Cz)	J Stark (US)/ M Navratilova (US)

US OPEN

	Men's Singles	Women's Singles	Men's Doubles
1988	M Wilander (Swe)	S Graf (FRG)	S Casal/E Sanchez (Spa)
1989	B Becker (FRG)	S Graf (FRG)	J McEnroe (US)/ M Woodforde (Aus)
1990	P Sampras (US)	G Sabatini (Arg)	P Aldrich/D Visser (SA)
1991	S Edberg (Swe)	M Seles (Yug)	J Fitzgerald (Aus)/ A Jarryd (Swe)
1992	S Edberg (Swe)	M Seles (Yug)	J Grabb/R Reneberg (US)
1993	P Sampras (US)	S Graf (Ger)	K Flach/R Leach (US)
1994	A Agassi (US)	A Sanchez-Vicario (Spa)	J Eltingh/ P Haarhuis (Neth)
1995	P Sampras (US)	S Graf (Ger)	T Woodbridge/ T Woodforde (Aus)

	Women's Doubles	Mixed Doubles
1988	G Fernandez/R White (US)	J Pugh (US)/J Novotna (Cz)
1989	M Navratilova (US)/ H Mandlikova (Aus)	S Cannon/R White (US)
1990	M Navratilova/ G Fernandez (US)	T Woodbridge/E Smylie (Aus)
1991	P Shriver (US)/N Zvereva (USSR)	T Nijssen/M Bollegraf (Neth)
1992	G Fernandez (US)/N Zvereva (CIS)	N Provis/M Woodforde (Aus)
1993	A Sanchez-Vicario (Spa)/ H Sukova (Cz Rep)	T Woodbridge (Aus)/ H Sukova (Cz Rep)
1994	A Sanchez-Vicario (Spa)/ J Novotna (Cz)	E Reinach (S Afr)/ P Galbraith (US)
1995	G Fernandez (US)/N Zvereva (Belarus)	M Lucena/M McGrath (US)

FRENCH OPEN

	Men's Singles	Women's Singles	Men's Doubles
1988	M Wilander (Swe)	S Graf (FRG)	A Gomez (Ecu)/ E Sanchez (Spa)
1989	M Chang (US)	A Sanchez (Spa)	J Grabb/P McEnroe (US)
1990	A Gomez (Ecu)	M Seles (Yug)	S Casal/E Sanchez (Spa)
1991	J Courier (US)	M Seles (Yug)	J Fitzgerald (Aus)/ A Jarryd (Swe)
1992	J Courier (US)	M Seles (Yug)	J Hlasek/M Rosset (Sui)
1993	S Bruguera (Spa)	S Graf (Ger)	L Jensen/M Jensen (US)
1994	S Bruguera (Spa)	A Sanchez-Vicario (Spa)	B Black (Zim)/ J Stark (US)
1995	T Muster (Aut)	S Graf (Ger)	J Eltingh/ P Haarhuis (Neth)

	Women's Doubles	Mixed Doubles
1988	M Navratilova/P Shriver (US)	J Lozano (Mex)/L McNeil (US)
1989	L Savchenko/N Zvereva (USSR)	T Nijssen/M Bollegraf (Neth)
1990	J Novotna/H Sukova (Cz)	J Lozano (Mex)/A Sanchez-Vicario (Spa)
1991	G Fernandez (US)/J Novotna (Cz)	C Suk/H Sukova (Cz)
1992	G Fernandez (US)/N Zvereva (CIS)	A Sanchez-Vicario (Spa)/ T Woodbridge (Aus)
1993	G Fernandez (US)/N Zvereva (Belarus)	A Olhovskiy/F Maniokova (Rus)
1994	G Fernandez (US)/N Zvereva (Belarus)	K Boogert/M Oosting (Neth)
1995	G Fernandez (US)/N Zvereva (Belarus)	L Neiland (Lat)/ M Woodforde (Aus)

AUSTRALIAN OPEN

	Men's Singles	Women's Singles	Men's Doubles
1988	M Wilander (Swe)	S Graf (FRG)	J Pugh/R Leach (US)
1989	I Lendl (Cz)	S Graf (FRG)	J Pugh/R Leach (US)
1990	I Lendl (Cz)	S Graf (FRG)	P Aldrich/D Visser (Spa)
1991	B Becker (Ger)	M Seles (Yug)	S Davis/D Pate (US)
1992	J Courier (US)	M Seles (Yug)	T Woodbridge/ M Woodforde (Aus)
1993	J Courier (US)	M Seles (Yug)	D Wisser (SA)/ L Warder (Aus)
1994	P Sampras (US)	S Graf (Ger)	J Eltingh/P Haarhuis (Neth)
1995	A Agassi (US)	M Pierce (Fr)	J Palmer/R Reneberg (US)
1996	B Becker (Ger)	M Seles (US)	S Edberg (Swe)/ P Korda (Cz)

	Women's Doubles	Mixed Doubles
1988	M Navratilova/P Shriver (US)	J Pugh (US)/J Novotna (Cz)
1989	M Navratilova/P Shriver (US)	J Pugh (US)/J Novotna (Cz)
1990	H Sukova/J Novotna (Cz)	J Pugh (US)/N Zvereva (USSR)
1991	P Fendick/M J Fernandez (US)	J Bates/J Durie (GB)
1992	A Sanchez-Vicario (Spa)/ H Sukova (Cz)	N Provis/M Woodforde (Aus)
1993	G Fernandez (US)/N Zvereva (Belarus)	T Woodbridge (Aus)/ A Sanchez-Vicario (Spa)
1994	G Fernandez (US)/N Zvereva (Belarus)	A Olhovskiy (Rus)/L Neiland (Lat)
1995	A Sanchez-Vicario (Spa)/ J Novotna (Cz)	R Leach (US)/ N Zvereva (Belarus)
1996	C Rubin (US)/ A Sanchez-Vicario (Spa)	L Neiland (Lat)/ M Woodforde (Aus)

HORSE RACING

	Grand National	**Cheltenham Gold Cup**	**1000 Guineas**
1988	Rhyme & Reason	Charter Party	Ravinella
1989	Little Polveir	Desert Orchid	Musical Bliss
1990	Mr Frisk	Norton's Coin	Salsabil
1991	Seagram	Garrison Savannah	Shadayid
1992	Party Politics	Cool Ground	Hatoof
1993	*declared void*	Jodami	Sayyedati
1994	Miinnehoma	The Fellow	Las Meninas
1995	Royal Athlete	Master Oats	Harayir

	2000 Guineas	**Oaks**	**Derby**
1988	Doyoun	Diminuendo	Kahyasi
1989	Nashwan	Snow Bride	Nashwan
1990	Tirol	Salsabil	Quest for Fame
1991	Mystiko	Jet Ski Lady	Generous
1992	Rodrigo de Triano	User Friendly	Dr Devious
1993	Zafonic	Intrepidity	Commander in Chief
1994	Mister Baileys	Balanchine	Erhaab
1995	Pennekamp	Moonshell	Lammtarra

	Ascot Gold Cup	**St Leger**
1988	Sadeem	Minster Son
1989	Sadeem	Michelozzo
1990	Ashal	Snurge
1991	Indian Queen	Toulon
1992	Drum Taps	User Friendly
1993	Drum Taps	Bob's Return
1994	Arcadian Heights	Moonax
1995	Double Trigger	Classic Cliché

MOTOR RACING

	World Champion	Constructors Championship	Indianapolis 500
1988	A Senna (Brazil)	McLaren-Honda	R Mears (US)
1989	A Prost (France)	McLaren-Honda	E Fittipaldi (Brazil)
1990	A Senna (Brazil)	McLaren-Honda	A Luyendyk (Neth)
1991	A Senna (Brazil)	McLaren-Honda	R Mears (US)
1992	N Mansell (GB)	Williams-Renault	A Unser Jnr (US)
1993	A Prost (France)	Williams-Renault	E Fittipaldi (Brazil)
1994	M Schumacher (Ger)	Williams-Renault	A Unser Jnr (US)
1995	M Schumacher (Ger)	Benetton-Renault	J Villeneuve (Can)

SNOOKER

	Embassy World Professional	Royal Liver Assurance	Skoda Grand Prix
1988	S Davis	D Mountjoy	S Davis
1989	S Davis	S Hendry	S Davis
1990	S Hendry	S Hendry	S Hendry
1991	J Parrot	J Parrot	S Hendry
1992	S Hendry	J White	J White
1993	S Hendry	J White	J White
1994	S Hendry	R O'Sullivan	P Ebden
1995	S Hendry	S Hendry	J Higgins

	Benson & Hedges Masters	British Open	International Open
1988	S Davis	S Hendry	S Davis
1989	S Hendry	T Meo	D Mountjoy
1990	S Hendry	B Chaperon (Can)	S James
1991	S Hendry	S Hendry	J White
1992	S Hendry	J White	S Davis

	Benson & Hedges Masters	British Open	International Open
1993	S Hendry	S Davis	S Hendry
1994	A McManus	R O'Sullivan	J Parrot
1995	R O'Sullivan	J Higgins	J Higgins

SKIING
SKI ALPINE CUP

	Men's Overall	Men's Downhill	Men's Slalom
1988	P Zurbriggen (Sui)	P Zurbriggen (Sui)	A Tomba (Ita)
1989	M Girardelli (Lux)	M Girardelli (Lux)	A Bittner (FRG)
1990	P Zurbriggen (Sui)	H Hoflehner (Aut)	A Bittner (FRG)
1991	M Girardelli (Lux)	F Heinzer (Sui)	M Girardelli (Lux)
1992	P Accola (Sui)	F Heinzer (Sui)	A Tomba (Ita)
1993	M Girardelli (Lux)	F Heinzer (Sui)	T Fogdoe (Swe)
1994	K Aamodt (Nor)	M Girardelli (Lux)	A Tomba (Ita)
1995	A Tomba (Ita)	L Alphand (Fra)	A Tomba (Ita)

	Men's Giant Slalom	Men's Super Giant Slalom
1988	A Tomba (Ita)	P Zurbriggen (Sui)
1989	O C Furuseth (Nor)	P Zurbriggen (Sui)
1990	O C Furuseth (Nor)	P Zurbriggen (Sui)
1991	A Tomba (Ita)	F Heinzer (Sui)
1992	A Tomba (Ita)	P Accola (Sui)
1993	K Aamodt (Nor)	K Aamodt (Nor)
1994	C Mayer (Aut)	J Thorson (Nor)
1995	A Tomba (Ita)	P Runggaldier (Ita)

	Women's Overall	Women's Downhill	Women's Slalom
1988	M Figini (Sui)	M Figini (Sui)	R Steiner (Aut)
1989	V Schneider (Sui)	M Figini (Sui)	V Schneider (Sui)
1990	P Kronberger (Aut)	K Gutensohn-Knopf (FRG)	V Schneider (Sui)
1991	P Kronberger (Aut)	C Bournissen (Sui)	P Krongberger (Aut)
1992	P Kronberger (Aut)	K Seizinger (Ger)	V Schneider (Sui)
1993	A Wachter (Aut)	K Seizinger (Ger)	V Schneider (Sui)
1994	V Schneider (Sui)	K. Seizinger (Ger)	V Schneider (Sui)
1995	V Schneider (Sui)	P Street (US)	V Schneider (Sui)

	Women's Giant Slalom	Women's Super Giant Slalom
1988	M Figini (Sui)	M Svet (Yug)
1989	C Merle (Fra)	V Schneider (Sui)
1990	C Merle (Fra)	A Wachter (Aut)
1991	C Merle (Fra)	V Schneider (Sui)
1992	C Merle (Fra)	C Merle (Fra)
1993	K Seizinger (Ger)	C Merle (Fra)
1994	K Seizinger (Ger)	A Wachter (Aut)
1995	V Schneider (Sui)	K Seizinger (Ger)

CYCLING

	Tour of Britain	Tour de France
1988	V Zhlanov (USSR)	P Delgado (Spa)
1989	B Walton (Canada)	G Lemond (US)
1990	S Sutton (Aus)	G Lemond (US)
1991	P Anderson (Aus)	M Indurain (Spa)
1992	C Henry (Ire)	M Indurain (Spa)
1993	P Anderson (Aus)	M Indurain (Spa)
1994	not run	M Indurain (Spa)
1995	not run	M Indurain (Spa)

ROWING

Oxford and Cambridge Boat Race

1988	Oxford	1992	Oxford
1989	Oxford	1993	Cambridge
1990	Oxford	1994	Cambridge
1991	Oxford	1995	Cambridge

BOWLS

World Indoors

1988	H Duff (Sco)
1989	R Corsie (Sco)
1990	J Price (Wales)
1991	R Corsie (Sco)
1992	I Schuback (Aus)
1993	R Corsie (Sco)
1994	A Thomson (Eng)
1995	A Thomson (Eng)

World Outdoors

1976	D Watson (SA)
1980	D Bryant (Eng)
1984	P Bellis (NZ)
1988	D Bryant (Eng)
1992	T Allcock (Eng)

AMERICAN FOOTBALL

Superbowl

1988	Washington Redskins
1989	San Francisco 49ers
1990	San Francisco 49ers
1991	New York Giants
1992	Washington Redskins
1993	Dallas Cowboys
1994	Dallas Cowboys
1995	Dallas Cowboys

YACHTING

	Americas Cup			Admiral's Cup
1977	*Courageous* (US)		1981	UK
1980	*Freedom* (US)		1983	W Germany
1983	*Australia II* (Aus)		1985	W Germany
1987	*Stars & Stripes* (US)		1987	New Zealand
1988	*Stars & Stripes* (US)		1989	UK
1992	*America 3* (US)		1991	France
1995	*Black Magic I* (NZ)		1993	Germany
			1995	Italy

CHESS

	World Men		World Women
1987	G Kasparov (USSR)	1986	M Chiburdanidze (USSR)
1990	G Kasparov (USSR)	1988	M Chiburdanidze (USSR)
1993	G Kasparov (USSR)	1991	X Jun (China)

General Interest

INTERNATIONAL TIME ZONES

The system was established in 1884 by agreement between the major countries. The meridian of longitude passing through Greenwich Observatory, London, was taken as the starting-point for 24 time zones (each,

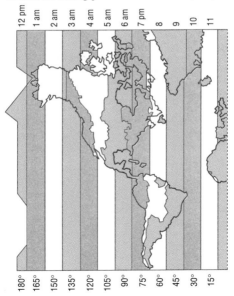

generally, representing 15° of longitude, the equivalent of 1 hour). There are 12 time zones west of Greenwich and 12 east. Within a time zone the time is the same throughout, but when crossing from one zone to another, the time changes by 1 hour. The world is divided into 23 full zones and 2 half zones, zone 12 east and zone 12 west, which are adjacent and separated by an imaginary line, the International Date

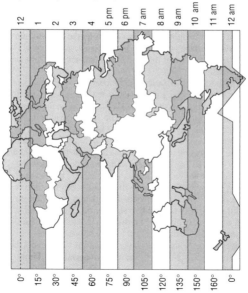

Line, halfway round the world from Greenwich. Thus a traveller crossing the line and heading west will lose a day, and if heading east will gain a day. See also **The International Date Line**.

Note: Several countries, including the UK, use Daylight Saving Time (DST) in order to maximize daylight time in summer. Clocks are put forward 1 hour in spring and back 1 hour in autumn. The above plan does not take account of DST adjustments.

THE INTERNATIONAL DATE LINE

This is an imaginary line which marks the place on the earth's surface where each new calendar day begins. The date on the west of the date line is one day later than on the east.

The International Date Line follows the 180th meridian for most of its length but is adjusted where necessary to avoid having two different calendar dates on the same day in a fairly small country. The 180th meridian is exactly halfway round the world from Greenwich, London.

The sun travels over 15° of the earth's surface each hour. For each 15° west of Greenwich, the time reverses one hour. At longitude 180° east the time is 12 hours ahead of Greenwich time. At longitude 180° west, the time is 12 hours behind Greenwich. Thus there is a 24-hour time difference between the two sides of the 180th meridian. A new date begins first on the western side of the date line. As the earth rotates on its axis, this new date sweeps westwards over the earth and the date covers the entire earth in 24 hours. See also **International Time Zones**.

CALENDARS

There are three main types of calendar:

Lunar Calendar

Most ancient calendars used the interval between successive full moons, the lunar month, as a measure of time. The lunar month is approximately 29½ days in length; thus a lunar year (12 x 29½) amounts to approximately 354 days. This means that its year is approximately 11 days shorter than the true solar year (approximately 365 days), and following it would cause the seasons to occur earlier and earlier each year. This makes the lunar calendar alone unsuitable for practical use.

Solar Calendar

The solar calendar adheres as closely as possible to the length of the solar year, but assumes a set length of month, thereby disregarding the lunar month. The solar year is 365.2422 days in length. Solar calendars use a normal year of 365 days and allow for the fraction (0.2422 days) by inserting an extra day every fourth year. The solar calendar has 4 critical points: 2 equinoxes and 2 solstices (see page 296). The fact that the equinoxes always occur on or about the same days each year establishes the accuracy of such a calendar.

Lunisolar Calendar

The lunisolar calendar is an attempt to recon
differences between the lunar and solar cale
lunar month of 29½ days becomes either a
day month (alternately), thus making 354

Additional months are inserted from time to time to
adjust the number of calendar days to the number of days
in a solar year. This is usually done by inserting a 13th
lunar month every 2 or 3 years, thus ensuring that the
seasons accord approximately with the calendar period.

CALENDARS IN USE TODAY
Gregorian Calendar

The Gregorian calendar is used almost exclusively
throughout the western world, and has been used in Great
Britain since 1752. It was calculated by Pope Gregory
XIII in the 1580s in an attempt to reform the Roman
Julian calendar which had become inaccurate and
confusing. As the true length of the solar year was then
known, Gregory simplified and adapted the Julian
calendar accordingly.

The Gregorian calendar has 12 months, 11 with either 30
or 31 days; February has 28 days and, every fourth year
(a leap year), 29 days. However, these adjustments are
still not quite enough to ensure absolute accuracy and so
in century years that cannot be divided by 400 (1700,
1800, 1900), February loses its leap year. The Gregorian
calendar is so accurate that the difference between
calendar and solar year is approximately 26 seconds.
This difference will increase by 0.53 second each century
because the solar year is gradually becoming shorter.

The western calendar is based on the year of Jesus
Christ's birth; dates before this event are noted BC (Before
Christ), and those after, as AD (Anno Domini, In the Year
ᶜ our Lord). Non-Christians often prefer BCE (Before
ᵗian Era) and CE (Christian Era).

Month	Derived from	Length (days)
January	*Januarius* (Latin). The Roman god, Janus, faces two ways and was often represented on doorways and archways.	31
February	*Februarius* (Latin). Taken from Februa, a purification rite which took place on February 15.	28 or 29
March	*Martius* (Latin). Mars was the Roman god of war.	31
April	*Aprilis* (Latin). Taken from *aperite* ('to open'), referring to the trees and flowers which are beginning to open.	30
May	*Maius* (Latin). Derived either from Maia, an obscure goddess, or from *maiores* ('elders'), referring to the period in which old people were honoured.	31
June	*Junius* (Latin). Derived either from the goddess Juno or *iuniores* ('young people'), indicating the period which was traditionally dedicated to young people.	30
July	*Julius* (Latin). Named after Gaius Julius Caesar, the Roman soldier and statesman.	31
August	*Augustus* (Latin). Named after Augustus Caesar, the first Roman Emperor.	31
September	*Septem* (Latin), meaning 'seven'; September was originally the seventh month in the Roman calendar.	30
October	*Octo* (Latin), meaning 'eight'; October was originally the eighth month in the Roman calendar.	31
November	*Novem* (Latin), meaning 'nine'; November was originally the ninth month in the Roman calendar.	30
December	*Decem* (Latin), meaning 'ten'; December was originally the tenth month in the Roman calendar.	31

The Christian Church Calendar is governed partly by the sun and partly by the moon. Immovable feasts such as Christmas are based on the solar calendar, whereas movable feasts, such as Ash Wednesday and Easter, vary each year according to the moon's phases.

Jewish Calendar

The Jewish calendar was begun, traditionally, at the moment of creation, 3,760 years and 3 months before the beginning of the Christian era. To find the Jewish year, add 3,760 years to the date in the Gregorian calendar. Thus, the Gregorian year 2000 will be 5760 in the Jewish calendar. As a lunisolar calendar, the Jewish calendar requires an extra month (Veadar) to be inserted seven times in a 19-year cycle; Veadar is inserted between Adar and Nisan and Adar is given 30 days instead of 29.

Month	Length (days)
Nisan	(March/April in Gregorian calendar) 30
Iyar	29
Sivan	30
Tammuz	29
Ab	30
Elul	29
Tishri	30
Heshvan	29/30
Kislev	29/30
Tebet	29
Shebat	30
Adar	29/30

Note: Nisan is the first month of the Jewish year, although years are numbered from Tishri, the seventh month.

Islamic Calendar

The Islamic calendar begins with Muhammad's flight from Mecca to Medina (the Hegira) in AD 622. As a lunar calendar the year is much shorter than the solar year and, as no adjustments are made, it moves fully backwards through the seasons over a period of 32½ years. Time is divided into 30-year cycles; during each cycle 19 years have the usual 354 days and 11 years take an extra day each. The Islamic year is based on the moon and has 12 months, alternately of 30 and 29 days.

Month	Length (days)
Muharram	30
Safar	29
Rabi I	30
Rabi II	29
Jumada I	30
Jumada II	29
Rajab	30
Shaban	29
Ramadan	30
Shawwal	29
Zulkadah	30
Zulhijjah	29*

* Takes an extra day in leap years.

Hindu Calendar

The Hindu calendar dates from about 1000 BC and was first used in India. It is a lunar calendar, so an additional month (Adhik) is incorporated every 30 months to remove the discrepancy between the lunar year (approximately 354 days) and the solar year (approximately 365 days). There are 12 months of 30 days each, divided into Shukla (the light fortnight) and Krishna (the dark fortnight).

Hindu Month Names

Chait'r (March/April in Gregorian calendar)	Vaishaakh
Jayshyth	Aashaadh
Shraawan	Bhaadrap'd
Aashwin	Kaartik
Maargasheersh	Paush
Maagh	Phaalgun

Chinese Calendar

The Chinese calendar began in 2637 BC when Emperor Huangdi is said to have invented it. It is a lunar calendar and years are calculated in cycles of 60 (e.g. 2000 is the 17th year in the 78th cycle).

There is a Buddhist belief that the Buddha invited all the animals to celebrate the New Year with him but only 12 came. As a reward the Buddha named a year after each of them in the order in which they arrived in his presence, with the rat first and the pig last.

The Chinese year is based on the moon and has 12 months, each beginning at a new moon with 29 or 30 days. A month is repeated seven times during each 19-year cycle so that the calendar stays approximately in line with the seasons. The Chinese New Year occurs at the second new moon after the beginning of winter; thus it is no earlier than 20 January and no later than 20 February.

Note: The official Chinese calendar now corresponds with the western system, but the old calendar is still used in Tibet, Hong Kong, Singapore, Malaysia and other parts of south-east Asia.

Animal	Year								
Rat	1900	1912	1924	1936	1948	1960	1972	1984	1996
Buffalo or Cow	1901	1913	1925	1937	1949	1961	1973	1985	1997
Tiger	1902	1914	1926	1938	1950	1962	1974	1986	1998
Rabbit	1903	1915	1927	1939	1951	1963	1975	1987	1999
Dragon	1904	1916	1928	1940	1952	1964	1976	1988	2000
Snake	1905	1917	1929	1941	1953	1965	1977	1989	2001
Horse	1906*	1918	1930	1942	1954	1966*	1978	1990	2002
Goat	1907	1919	1931	1943	1955	1967	1979	1991	2003
Monkey	1908	1920	1932	1944	1956	1968	1980	1992	2004
Rooster or Chicken	1909	1921	1933	1945	1957	1969	1981	1993	2005
Dog	1910	1922	1934	1946	1958	1970	1982	1994	2006
Pig	1911	1923	1935	1947	1959	1971	1983	1995	2007

* Called Fire Horse once every 60 years

FRENCH REVOLUTIONARY CALENDAR

The French Revolutionary Calendar was an attempt by the First French Republic to reform the Gregorian calendar in line with revolutionary principles. It was adopted in 1793 and abandoned in 1805.

Vendémiaire (Month of Grape Harvest)	23 September–22 October
Brumaire (Month of Mist)	23 October–21 November
Frimaire (Frosty Month)	22 November–21 December
Nivôse (Snowy Month)	22 December–20 January
Pluviôse (Rainy Month)	21 January–19 February
Ventôse (Windy Month)	20 February–21 March
Germinal (Month of Buds)	22 March–20 April
Floréal (Month of Flowers)	21 April–20 May
Prairial (Month of Meadows)	21 May–19 June
Messidor (Month of Harvest)	20 June–19 July
Thermidor (Month of Heat)	20 July–18 August
Fructidor (Month of Fruit)	19 August–22 September

SOLSTICE

The time when the sun is farthest from the equator and appears to stand still. Occurs twice yearly:

Winter Solstice (around 22 December) = shortest day
Summer Solstice (around 21 June) = longest day

EQUINOX

The time when the sun crosses the equator and day and night are equal. Occurs twice yearly:

Spring (Vernal) Equinox (around 21 March)
Autumnal Equinox (around 23 September)

QUARTER DAYS (ENGLAND, WALES AND NORTHERN IRELAND)

The four days of the year when certain payments become due.

Lady Day	25 March
Midsummer	24 June
Michaelmas	29 September
Christmas	25 December

SCOTTISH TERM DAYS

A division of the academic year when schools, colleges or universities are in session, and one of the periods of time during which sessions of courts of law are held.

Candlemas 2 February	Feast of the Purification of the Virgin Mary and the day on which church candles are blessed.
Whit Sunday 7th Sunday after Easter	Commemorates the descent of the Holy Spirit after Easter (movable) on the day of Pentecost. Whit (or white) Sunday was so called because white robes were worn on that day.
Lammas 1 August	Feast commemorating St Peter's miraculous delivery from prison. Formerly observed in England as a Harvest Festival, when loaves made from the first ripe corn were consecrated. (Origin: Old English *hlafmaesse*, 'loaf mass'.)
Martinmas 11 November	Feast of St Martin, formerly day for hiring servants and slaughtering cattle to be salted for the winter.

BIRTHSTONES, ASTROLOGICAL SIGNS AND NAMES

Month	Gem	Characteristic
January	Garnet	Constancy
February	Amethyst	Sincerity
March	Aquamarine Bloodstone	Courage
April	Diamond	Innocence
May	Emerald	Love
June	Pearl, Alexandrite Moonstone	Health
July	Ruby	Contentment
August	Peridot Sardonyx	Married happiness
September	Sapphire	Clear thinking
October	Opal Tourmaline	Hope
November	Topaz	Faithfulness
December	Turquoise Zircon	Wealth

Corresponding Astrological (Zodiac) Sign*

♒	Aquarius (20 January–18 February)
♓	Pisces (19 February–20 March)
♈	Aries (21 March–19 April)
♉	Taurus (20 April–20 May)
♊	Gemini (21 May–20 June)
♋	Cancer (21 June–22 July)
♌	Leo (23 July–22 August)
♍	Virgo (23 August–22 September)
♎	Libra (23 September–22 October)
♏	Scorpio (23 October–21 November)
♐	Sagittarius (22 November–21 December)
♑	Capricorn (22 December–19 January)

* Astrological signs do not correspond exactly with the beginning and end of the month; birthdate should be the guide to the appropriate gemstone.

WEDDING ANNIVERSARIES

Year	Gift
1	Paper, plastics, furniture
2	Cotton, china
3	Leather or artificial leather articles
4	Linen, silk or synthetic silks
5	Wood and decorative articles for the home
6	Iron
7	Wood, copper, brass
8	Bronze, electrical appliances
9	Pottery, china, glass, crystal
10	Tin, aluminium
11	Steel
12	Linen, silk, nylon
13	Lace
14	Ivory, agate
15	Crystal, glass
20	China, small items of furniture
25	Silver
30	Pearls or personal gifts
35	Coral, jade
40	Rubies, garnets
45	Sapphires, tourmalines,
50	Gold
55	Emeralds, turquoises
60, 75	Diamonds, gold

ORDERS OF PRECEDENCE

The Peerage

Title Royal Duke/Duchess
Style His Royal Highness the Duke of . . . /
Her Royal Highness the Duchess of . . .
Addressed as Sir or, formally, May it please your Royal Highness

Title Archbishop
Style The Most Reverend His Grace the Lord Archbishop of . . .
Addressed as My Lord Archbishop or Your Grace

Title Duke/Duchess
Style His Grace the Duke of . . . /
Her Grace the Duchess of . . .
Addressed as My Lord Duke/
Your Grace; Dear Madam/Duchess*

Title Marquess/Marchioness
Style The Most Honourable the Marquess of . . . /
The Most Honourable the Marchioness of . . .
Addressed as My Lord/My Lord; Madam/Lady*

Title Earl/Countess
Style The Right Honourable The Earl of . . . /
The Right Honourable the Countess of . . .
Addressed as My Lord/My Lord;
Madam/Madam*

Title Viscount/Viscountess
Style The Right Honourable the Viscount . . . /
The Right Honourable the Viscountess . . .
Addressed as My Lord/My Lady; Madam/Lady*

Title Bishop
Style The Right Reverend the Lord Bishop of . . .
Addressed as My Lord

Title Baron/Baroness
Style The Right Honourable the Lord . . . /
The Right Honourable the Lady . . .
Addressed as My Lord/Lord; My Lady/Lady*

* This section shows the correct forms of address for letters (formal)
and when speaking (formal)

ORDERS OF CHIVALRY
Title The Most Noble Order of the Garter
Date 1348
Abbrev. KG
Ribbon Garter blue
Motto Honi soit qui mal y pense (Shame on him who thinks evil of it)
Limit 24

Title The Most Ancient and Most Noble Order of the Thistle
Date Revived 1687
Abbrev. KT
Ribbon Green
Motto Nemo me impune lacessit (No one provokes me with impunity)
Limit 16

Title The Most Honourable Order of the Bath
Date 1725
Abbrev. GCB, KCB, DCB, CB
Ribbon Crimson
Motto Tria juncta in uno (Three joined in one)

Title The Order of Merit
Date 1902
Abbrev. OM
Ribbon Blue and crimson
Limit 24

Title The Most Exalted Order of the Star of India
Date 1861
Abbrev. GCSI, KCSI, CSI
Ribbon Light blue with white edges
Motto Heaven's light our guide
Note: No conferments have been made since 1947.

Title The Most Distinguished Order of St Michael and St George
Date 1818
Abbrev. GCMG, KCMG, DCMG, CMG
Ribbon Saxe blue with scarlet centre
Motto Auspicum melioris aevi (Token of a better age)

Title The Most Eminent Order of the Indian Empire
Date 1868
Abbrev. GCIE, KCIE, CIE
Ribbon Imperial purple
Motto Imperatricis auspiciis (Under the auspices of the Empress)
Note: No conferments have been made since 1947.

Title The Distinguished Service Order
Date 1886
Abbrev. DSO
Ribbon Red with blue edges

Title The Imperial Service Order
Date 1902
Abbrev. ISO
Ribbon Crimson with blue centre

Title The Royal Victorian Chain
Date 1902

Title The Imperial Order of the Crown of India (for ladies only)
Date 1877
Abbrev. CI
Badge Royal cipher surmounted by heraldic crown with bow of
light blue watered ribbon, edged white
Note: No conferments have been made since 1947.

Title The Royal Victorian Order
Date 1896
Abbrev. GCVO, KCVO, DCVO, CVO, LVO, MVO
Ribbon Blue, with white and red edges
Motto Victoria

Title The Most Excellent Order of the British Empire
Date 1917
Abbrev. GVE, DBE, CBE, OBE, MBE
Ribbon Rose pink edged with light grey; military division has
vertical grey stripe in centre, civil division does not
Motto For God and the Empire

Title The Order of the Companions of Honour
Date 1917
Abbrev. CH
Ribbon Carmine with gold edges
Limit 65

Baronetage and Knightage
Title Baronet
Style 'Sir' before forename and surname, followed by 'Bt'
Wife 'Lady' followed by surname

Title Knight
Style 'Sir' before forename and surname, followed by 'Bt' (if applicable), plus appropriate initials (KGC, KC, etc.)
Wife 'Lady' plus surname

PRINCIPAL BRITISH ORDERS AND DECORATIONS IN ORDER OF PRECEDENCE

Title	Date of Institution	Abbreviation
Knight of the Garter	1348	KG
Knight of the Thistle	809	KT
Knight of St Patrick	1783*	KP
Knight Grand Cross of the Bath	1725	GCB
Order of Merit	1902	OM
Knight Grand Commander, Star of India	1861	GCSI
Knight Grand Cross, St Michael and St George	1818	GCMG
Knight Grand Commander, Order of the Indian Empire	1878*	GCIE
Crown of India (Ladies)	1878*	CI
Knight Grand Cross, Victorian Order	1896	GCVO
Knight Grand Cross, British Empire	1917	GBE
Companions of Honour	1917	CH
Knight Commander, Bath	1725	KCB
Knight Commander, Star of India	1861	KCSI
Knight Commander, St Michael and St George	1818	KCMG
Knight Commander, Indian Empire	1878*	KCIE
Knight Commander, Victorian Order	1896	KCVO
Knight Commander, British Empire	1917	KBE
Knights Bachelor	**	Kt.
Companion, Bath	1725	CB
Companion, Star of India	1861	CSI
Companion, St Michael and St George	1818	CMG

Companion, Indian Empire	1878*	CIE
Commander, Victorian Order	1896	CVO
Commander, British Empire	1917	CBE
Companion, Distinguished Service Order	1886	DSO
Order of the British Empire	1917	OBE
Companion, Imperial Service Order	1902	ISO
Member, British Empire	1917	MBE
Indian Order of Merit	1837*	IOM
Order of British India	1837*	OBI

* Obsolete

** Not an order; entitles the recipient to be called 'Sir' but knighthood cannot be passed on to heirs. Awarded for distinguished service.

DECORATIONS FOR GALLANTRY AND DISTINGUISHED SERVICE

Title	Date of Institution	Abbreviation
Victoria Cross	1856	VC
George Cross	1940	GC
Conspicuous Gallantry Cross	1995	CGC
Distinguished Service Order	1886	DSO
Distinguished Service Cross	1901	DSC
Military Cross	1914	MC
Distinguished Flying Cross	1918	DFC
Air Force Cross	1918	AFC
Albert Medal	1866	AM
Distinguished Conduct Medal (army)	1845	DCM
Conspicuous Gallantry Medal (navy & RAF)	1855, 1874	CGM
George Medal	1940	GM
Distinguished Service Medal (navy)	1914	DSM
Military Medal	1916	MM
Distinguished Flying Medal	1918	DFM
British Empire Medal	1917*	BEM

CROSSES USED AS CHARGES IN HERALDRY

a

b

c

d

e

f

g

h

i

j

a Patonce
b Flory
c Floretty
d Moline
e Crosslet or cross botonny

f Cross crosslet fitchy
g Potent
h Paty or Formy
i The Tau cross
j Maltese cross

THE ARMED FORCES
The Army

 Field Marshal

 General (Gen)

 Lieutenant-General (Lt-Gen)

 Major-General (Maj-Gen)

 Brigadier (Brig)

 Colonel (Col)

 Lieutenant-Colonel (Lt-Col)

 Major (Maj)

 Captain (Capt)

 Lieutenant (Lt)

 Second Lieutenant (2nd Lt)

Warrant Officer
Staff Sergeant
Sergeant
Corporal
Lance Corporal
Private

The Royal Navy

Admiral of the Fleet

Admiral (Adm)

Vice-Admiral (Vice-Adm)

Rear-Admiral (Rear-Adm)

Commodore (1st and 2nd Class) (Cdre)

Captain (Capt)

Commander (Cdr)

Lieutenant-Commander (Lt-Cdr)

Lieutenant (Lt)

Sub-Lieutenant (Sub-Lt)

Midshipman

Fleet Chief Petty Officer
Chief Petty Officer
Petty Officer
Leading Rating (or Seaman)
Able Rating (or Seaman)
Junior Rating (or Seaman)

The Royal Air Force

Marshal of the RAF

Squadron Leader (Squ Ldr)

Air Chief Marshal

Flight Lieutenant (Flt Lt)

Air Marshal

Flying Officer (FO)

Air Vice-Marshal

Pilot Officer (PO)

Air Commodore (Air Cdre)

Acting Pilot Officer
Warrant Officer
Flight Sergeant
Sergeant
Corporal
Junior Technician
Senior Aircraftman
Leading Aircraftman
Aircraftman

Group Captain (Gp Capt)

Wing Commander (Wg Cdr)

THE POLICE

 Commissioner

 Deputy and Assistant commissioner

 Deputy Assistant commissioner

 Commander

 Chief Superintendent

 Superintendent

 Chief Inspector

 Inspector

 Sergeant

 Constable

Published by courtesy of the Metropolitan Police Service

THE LANGUAGE OF FLOWERS

Symbolic meanings have been attributed to flowers for hundreds of years. The Victorians in particular were adept at contriving posies and sending carefully chosen Valentine cards bearing 'hidden' messages in the choice of flowers.

Flower/plant	Symbolizes/represents
Almond blossom	Sweetness, delicacy
Anemone	Withered hopes
Aster	Afterthought
Bayleaf	Loyalty
Buttercup	Ingratitude
Carnation	Betrothal, marriage, eternal love
Carnation, striped	Refusal
Chrysanthemum, red	Declaration of love
Chrysanthemum, white	Truth
Chrysanthemum, yellow	Rejected love
Columbine	Deserted lovers, folly
Cornflower	Delicacy
Daffodil	Regard
Forget-me-not	True love
Geranium, lemon or scented	Recalling a meeting
Heliotrope	Love and devotion
Hyacinth	Playfulness
Lavender	Distrust
Lily, white	Purity
Lily, yellow	Falsehood
Marigold, French	Jealousy
Periwinkle, blue	Recent friendship
Periwinkle, white	Pleasant memories
Phlox	Agreement
Pink	'You are always lovely'
Poppy, red	Consolation

Rose, red	Love, declaration of
Rose, yellow	Jealousy
Rosemary	Remembering sweet moments together
Sage	Domestic virtue
Snapdragon	Presumption
Stocks	Lasting beauty
Sweet pea	Delicate pleasure
Tulip, red	Declaration of love
Tulip, yellow	Hopeless love

Symbolizes/represents	Flower/plant
Afterthought	Aster
Agreement	Phlox
Beauty, lasting	Stocks
Betrothal	Carnation
Consolation	Poppy, red
Declaration of love	Chrysanthemum, red; rose, red; tulip, red
Delicacy	Almond blossom; cornflower
Deserted lovers	Columbine
Devotion and love	Heliotrope
Distrust	Lavender
Domestic Virtue	Sage
Eternal love	Carnation
Falsehood	Lily, yellow
Folly	Columbine
Friendship, recent	Periwinkle, blue
Hopeless love	Tulip, yellow
Hopes, withered	Anemone
Ingratitude	Buttercup
Jealousy	Marigold, French; rose, yellow
Lasting beauty	Stocks
Love	Rose, red

Love and devotion	Heliotrope
Love, declaration of	Chrysanthemum, red; rose, red; tulip, red
Love, eternal	Carnation
Love, hopeless	Tulip, yellow
'Lovely, you are always'	Pink
Love, rejected	Chrysanthemum, yellow
Lovers, deserted	Columbine
Love, true	Forget-me-not
Loyalty	Bayleaf
Marriage	Carnation
Meeting, recalling a	Geranium, lemon or scented
Memories, pleasant	Periwinkle, white
Playfulness	Hyacinth
Pleasant memories	Periwinkle, white
Pleasure, delicate	Sweet pea
Presumption	Snapdragon
Purity	Lily, white
Recalling a meeting	Geranium, lemon or scented
Recent friendship	Periwinkle, blue
Refusal	Carnation, striped
Regard	Daffodil
Rejected love	Chrysanthemum, white
Remembering sweet moments together	Rosemary
Sweetness	Almond Blossom
True love	Forget-me-not
Truth	Chrysanthemum, white
Virtue, domestic	Sage
'War', declaration of	Tansy
Withered hopes	Anemone
'You are always lovely'	Pink

THE KNIGHTS OF THE ROUND TABLE
King Arthur's knights were so-called because of the large, circular table around which they sat and which gave precedence to none, save the king. Popularly thought to have numbered 12, some sources indicate there were many more, even as many as 150. The following list gives the names of the best known:

Sir Kay	Sir Bedivere
Sir Gareth	Sir Gawain
Sir Lancelot du Lac	Sir Tristan de Lyonnais
Sir Galahad	Sir Perceval
Sir Bors	Sir Ector
Sir Tarquin	Sir Lionel
Sir Mordred*	

* Mordred was Arthur's son and ultimately responsible for his downfall.

THE FOUR TEMPERAMENTS OR HUMOURS
These were thought to represent the dominant characteristics of human beings, an idea first put forward by Aristotle. It was recognized that individuals are a mixture of all four traits, but the theory held that every person showed one of the four temperaments as a ruling quality. The humours are the four principal bodily fluids and each of the temperaments is characterized by the prevailing influence of one of the humours.

Temperament	Humour
Sanguine	Blood
Melancholic	Black bile
Choleric	Yellow bile
Lethargic or phlegmatic	Phlegm

THE SEVEN LIBERAL ARTS
This classification dates from the Middle Ages and was taken to be the basis of secular education.

The Trivium – Logic, Grammar, Rhetoric
The Quadrivium – Arithmetic, Geometry, Astronomy, Music

THE SIX WIVES OF HENRY VIII
1 Catherine of Aragon (divorced)
2 Anne Boleyn (beheaded)
3 Jane Seymour (died)
4 Anne of Cleves (divorced)
5 Catherine Howard (beheaded)
6 Catherine Parr (survived)

THE THREE GRACES (Greek Mythology)
Three sister goddesses, givers of charm and beauty.

Aglaia
Euphrosyne
Thalia; one of the nine Muses

THE NINE MUSES (Greek Mythology)
Nine sister goddesses, daughters of Zeus and Mnemosyne, each regarded as protectress of a different art or science.

Name	Muse of
Calliope	Epic Poetry
Clio	History
Erato	Love Poetry
Euterpe	Lyric Poetry and Music
Melpomene	Tragedy

Polyhmnia	Singing, Mime and Sacred Dance
Terpsichore	Dance and Choral Song
Thalia	Comedy and Pastoral Poetry; one of the Three Graces
Urania	Astronomy

THE LABOURS OF HERCULES

To slay the Nemean lion and bring back its skin

To kill the Lernean Hydra

To catch and retain the Arcadian stag (Ceryneian hind)

To destroy the Erymanthean boar

To cleanse the stables of King Augeas, King of Elis

To destroy the cannibal birds of Lake Stymphalis

To capture the Cretan bull

To catch the horses of the Thracian Diomedes who fed them on human flesh

To get possession of the girdle of Hippolyte, Queen of the Amazons, and bring it to Admete, daughter of Eurystheus

To capture the oxen of the monster Geryon

To get possession of the apples of the Hesperides

To bring up from the infernal regions the three-headed dog, Cerberus

THE SEVEN VIRTUES

Faith	Prudence	Fortitude
Hope	Justice	Temperance
Charity		

The first three are called the Holy Virtues.

THE SEVEN WONDERS OF THE ANCIENT WORLD

Pyramids of Egypt   Hanging Gardens of Babylon
Statue of Zeus at Olympia   Temple of Artemis at Ephesus
Mausoleum of Halicarnassus   Colossus of Rhodes
Pharos (lighthouse) of Alexandria

THE SEVEN SEAS

North Pacific Ocean   South Pacific Ocean
North Atlantic Ocean   South Atlantic Ocean
Arctic Ocean   Antarctic Ocean
Indian Ocean

THE SEVEN DEADLY SINS

Pride   Covetousness   Lust   Envy
Gluttony   Anger   Sloth

THE TWELVE DAYS OF CHRISTMAS
(Traditional English carol)

My true love sent to me
A partridge in a pear tree,
Two turtle doves,
Three French hens,
Four calling birds,
Five gold rings,
Six geese a-laying,
Seven swans a-swimming,
Eight maids a-milking,
Nine ladies dancing,
Ten lords a-leaping,
Eleven pipers piping,
Twelve drummers drumming.